641.552 AFF
The affordable feasts
collection ... ... ien
C... ... Kitc

ll0567490

LC JUN 2013
LU MAY 2014
Ri FA MAY 2018
WK MAR 2016
RE FEB 2017
MI APR 18

The
AFFORDABLE
FEASTS *Collection*

TRANSCONTINENTAL BOOKS
5800 Saint-Denis St.
Suite 900
Montreal, Que. H2S 3L5
Telephone: 514-273-1066
Toll-free: 1-800-565-5531
canadianliving.com

Bibliothèque et Archives nationales du
Québec and Library and Archives Canada
cataloguing in publication

Main entry under title:
The affordable feasts collection:
budget-friendly family meals
"Canadian living".
Includes index.
ISBN 970-0-9077474-3-3
1. Low budget cooking. 2. Quick and easy
cooking. 3. Cookbooks. I. Canadian Living
Test Kitchen. II. Title: Canadian living.

TX652.A33 2013   641.5'52
C2012-942166-9

Project editor: Tina Anson Mine
Copy editor: Julia Armstrong
Indexer: Beth Zabloski
Art director and designer: Chris Bond

All rights reserved. Reproduction in whole
or in part by any means whatsoever,
whether graphic, electronic or mechanical,
is strictly forbidden without the written
permission of the publisher.

Printed in Canada
© Transcontinental Books, 2013
Legal deposit – 1st quarter 2013
National Library of Quebec
National Library of Canada
ISBN 978-0-9877474-3-3

We acknowledge the financial support of
our publishing activity by the Government
of Canada through the Canada Book Fund.

For information on special rates for
corporate libraries and wholesale
purchases, please call 1-866-800-2500.

Canadian Living

The
AFFORDABLE
FEASTS *Collection*

Budget-friendly family meals

BY THE CANADIAN LIVING TEST KITCHEN

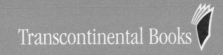

Transcontinental Books

Spaghetti With Mussel
Marinara Sauce, page 193

It makes sense to spend your food dollars wisely – and not just in hard times. Whether you're a starving student, working hard and watching every penny, or you're financially cosy and planning your next trip to Fiji, it's always a good idea to choose less expensive groceries and prepare them deliciously. Sure, it's easy and it lets you spend your hard-earned cash in other areas of your life, but it's also smart and socially responsible to avoid wasting money and food.

Like many of you, I grew up in a working-class home. My mother, a busy nurse, prepared a steady rotation of dinners, nearly all of them based on ground beef. Monday was spaghetti, Tuesday was leftovers, Wednesday was meat loaf…. You get the idea. When I moved out, I didn't want to eat ground beef again for a year!

What my mum didn't know is that some simple choices made at the grocery store could have kept our family from getting tired of the usual ground beef. So many tasty foods are inexpensive – and they're the base for some of the most delicious dishes that The Test Kitchen has created over the last 35-plus years.

In this book, we've included recipes that use all of our favourite budget-friendly ingredients (including ground meat!) and lots of bonus tips to help you save money and reduce kitchen waste. Whether you're making a Tuesday night family supper or a chic dinner party meal, you can make wise choices and no one will be the wiser. And with the variety of Tested-Till-Perfect recipes in this book, I can assure you that no one will be getting tired of anything.

Eat well!

– Annabelle Waugh,
food director

chapter one
chapter two
chapter three
chapter four
chapter five

Red Meat

8

White Meat

56

Eggs, Beans & Tofu

106

Pasta, Noodles & Rice

154

Hearty Vegetables

200

Index

247

Chunky Chili con Carne,
page 12

chapter one

Red Meat

Hearty Beef Stew

Beef stew is one of the most requested *Canadian Living* recipes. If you're making the slow cooker variation and time is of the essence, you can skip browning the meat and just put it directly into the slow cooker.

1½ lb (675 g) **stewing beef cubes**

½ cup **all-purpose flour**

¼ tsp each **salt** and **pepper**

1 tbsp **vegetable oil**

2 **onions,** cut in wedges

1½ tsp **dried Italian herb seasoning**

2 **bay leaves**

1 can (28 oz/796 mL) **whole tomatoes**

2 cups chopped peeled **sweet potatoes**

2 **potatoes,** peeled and chopped

2 ribs **celery,** chopped

1¾ cups **sodium-reduced beef broth**

1 cup **frozen peas**

Trim and cut beef into 1-inch (2.5 cm) cubes. In plastic bag, shake together beef, flour, salt and pepper; reserving remaining flour mixture, remove beef. In Dutch oven, heat 2 tsp of the oil over medium-high heat; brown beef, in batches. Transfer to plate.

Add remaining oil, onions, Italian herb seasoning, bay leaves and reserved flour mixture to pan; cook over medium-low heat, scraping up browned bits, for 5 minutes. Return beef and any accumulated juices to pan.

Using potato masher, crush tomatoes; add to pan along with sweet potatoes, potatoes, celery and broth. Bring to boil; cover and simmer over medium-low heat or cook in 325°F (160°C) oven, stirring occasionally, until beef is tender, about 2 hours. Uncover and cook until slightly thickened, about 15 minutes.

Stir in peas. Discard bay leaves.

change it up!

Slow Cooker Hearty Beef Stew

Increase broth to 2½ cups. In large skillet, heat oil over medium-high heat; brown beef, in batches. Transfer to plate. In 18- to 24-cup (4.5 to 6 L) slow cooker, crush tomatoes with potato masher. Add onions, sweet potatoes, potatoes, celery, bay leaves, Italian herb seasoning and beef; pour in 2 cups of the broth. Cover and cook on low until beef and vegetables are tender, 10 to 12 hours. Add peas, salt and pepper. Whisk flour with remaining broth; stir into stew. Cook, covered, until thickened, about 15 minutes. Discard bay leaves.

Makes 6 servings. PER SERVING: about 407 cal, 28 g pro, 15 g total fat (5 g sat. fat), 40 g carb, 5 g fibre, 67 mg chol, 565 mg sodium, 995 mg potassium. % RDI: 9% calcium, 36% iron, 77% vit A, 52% vit C, 28% folate.

CANADIAN CLASSIC

Chunky Chili con Carne

Chili without beans is as traditional as the popular bean-and-beef combo. But you can add pinto or red kidney beans (one 19-oz/540 mL can, drained and rinsed) if you just can't imagine your chili without them.

2 lb (900 g) **stewing beef cubes**

1 tbsp **vegetable oil**

2 **onions,** chopped

2 cloves **garlic,** slivered

2 tbsp **chili powder**

2 tsp **ground cumin**

1 tsp each **cinnamon** and **dried oregano**

1 tsp **granulated sugar**

¼ tsp **salt**

1 can (28 oz/796 mL) **whole tomatoes**

1 cup **beef broth**

2 tbsp **red wine vinegar**

2 tbsp **tomato paste**

Trim and cut beef into bite-size pieces. In Dutch oven, heat half of the oil over medium-high heat; brown beef, in batches and adding remaining oil as necessary.

Return all beef to pan. Add onions, garlic, chili powder, cumin, cinnamon, oregano, sugar and salt; cook over medium heat until onions are softened, about 5 minutes.

Add tomatoes, broth, vinegar and tomato paste, mashing tomatoes with back of spoon; bring to boil. Cover and simmer over low heat, stirring occasionally, for 1 hour.

Uncover and simmer until thickened, about 1¼ hours. *(Make-ahead: Let cool for 30 minutes. Freeze in airtight containers for up to 1 month.)*

Makes 8 servings. PER SERVING: about 255 cal, 27 g pro, 12 g total fat (4 g sat. fat), 10 g carb, 2 g fibre, 63 mg chol, 408 mg sodium. % RDI: 6% calcium, 26% iron, 13% vit A, 30% vit C, 8% folate.

Ground Beef Chili

Simple, pantry-staple ingredients make this dish a perennial winner. Save some for later, because the leftovers taste even better the next day.

1 tbsp **vegetable oil**

3 **onions,** chopped

4 cloves **garlic,** minced

2 lb (900 g) **medium ground beef** or lean ground beef

3 tbsp **chili powder**

1¼ tsp **ground cumin**

1 tsp **ground coriander**

1 tsp **dried oregano**

1 tsp **salt**

¼ tsp **pepper**

¼ tsp **cayenne pepper** (optional)

1 can (28 oz/796 mL) **whole tomatoes**

½ cup **bottled strained tomatoes** (passata)

1 can (19 oz/540 mL) **red kidney beans,** drained and rinsed

In Dutch oven, heat oil over medium heat; cook onions and garlic, stirring occasionally, until golden, 8 to 10 minutes.

Add beef; cook, breaking up with spoon, until browned. Stir in chili powder, cumin, coriander, oregano, salt, pepper, and cayenne pepper (if using); cook for 1 minute.

Using potato masher, crush whole tomatoes; add to pan along with strained tomatoes, ½ cup water and beans. Bring to boil; reduce heat, cover and simmer for 20 minutes. Uncover and cook for 10 minutes.

Makes 6 to 8 servings. PER EACH OF 8 SERVINGS: about 373 cal, 26 g pro, 21 g total fat (8 g sat. fat), 20 g carb, 6 g fibre, 68 mg chol, 696 mg sodium, 747 mg potassium. % RDI: 8% calcium, 34% iron, 10% vit A, 28% vit C, 18% folate.

CLASSIC
WITH
A TWIST

Taco Pizza

Here are two of everyone's favourite family dinners wrapped into one delicious package. Store-bought pizza dough is convenient and affordable, but when you have time, save even more money by making Multigrain Pizza Dough (below).

12 oz (340 g) **lean ground beef**

1 small **onion,** chopped

2 cloves **garlic,** minced

1 tbsp **chili powder**

1 tsp **dried oregano**

¼ tsp each **salt** and **pepper**

1½ lb (675 g) **whole wheat pizza dough** or Multigrain Pizza Dough (below)

1 cup **salsa** or pizza sauce

1 cup shredded **extra-old Cheddar cheese**

2 cups shredded **lettuce**

1 **tomato,** chopped

Half **avocado,** pitted, peeled and diced

¼ cup sliced **black olives** (optional)

¼ cup **light sour cream**

In large nonstick skillet, cook beef over medium-high heat, breaking up with spoon, until browned, about 5 minutes.

Drain fat from pan; add onion, garlic, chili powder, oregano, salt and pepper. Cook over medium heat, stirring often, until onion is softened, about 3 minutes.

On lightly floured surface, divide dough into quarters; shape each into disc. Roll out each into 8-inch (20 cm) oval; place on greased large baking sheet. Spread each with salsa; sprinkle with meat mixture, then cheese. Bake in bottom third of 425°F (220°C) oven until cheese is bubbly and crust is golden, 20 to 25 minutes.

Top each pizza with lettuce, tomato, avocado, olives (if using) and sour cream.

make your own!

Multigrain Pizza Dough

In bowl, combine 1¾ cups multigrain bread flour, 1½ cups all-purpose flour, ¼ cup mixed seeds (such as flax, sunflower and sesame), 2 tsp quick-rising (instant) dry yeast and 1 tsp salt. Gradually stir in 1¼ cups hot (120°F/50°C) water and 1 tbsp extra-virgin olive oil until ragged dough forms. On lightly floured surface, knead dough until smooth and elastic, about 8 minutes. Place in greased bowl; turn to grease all over. Cover and let rise in warm draft-free place until doubled in bulk, 1 hour. *(Make-ahead: Refrigerate unrisen dough and let rise for 24 hours. Or freeze in plastic bag for up to 1 month; let thaw and rise in refrigerator overnight.)* **Makes about 1½ lb (675 g) dough.**

Makes 4 to 6 servings. PER EACH OF 6 SERVINGS: about 509 cal, 29 g pro, 20 g total fat (8 g sat. fat), 64 g carb, 12 g fibre, 53 mg chol, 1,217 mg sodium. % RDI: 22% calcium, 32% iron, 13% vit A, 12% vit C, 16% folate.

Beef & Cabbage Soup

This simple supper soup is a great way to use up leftover cooked rice. Cabbage keeps well, so chop an entire head while you're prepping for this soup and add the remainder to salads all week to give them a nutritious crunch.

12 oz (340 g) **lean ground beef**

1 tbsp **vegetable oil**

1 **onion,** diced

1 clove **garlic,** minced

2 **bay leaves**

½ tsp each **dried thyme, dried marjoram** and **salt**

¼ tsp **pepper**

Pinch **ground cloves**

3 cups chopped **cabbage**

2 **carrots,** halved lengthwise and sliced

2 ribs **celery,** sliced

3 cups **sodium-reduced beef broth**

¼ cup **tomato paste**

1 cup **cooked rice**

Lemon wedges

In large saucepan, cook beef over medium-high heat, breaking up with spoon, until browned. With slotted spoon, transfer to bowl.

Drain fat from pan; heat oil over medium heat. Cook onion, garlic, bay leaves, thyme, marjoram, salt, pepper and cloves, stirring often, until onion is softened, about 5 minutes. Stir in cabbage, carrots and celery; cook, stirring, for 3 minutes.

Add broth, 3 cups water and tomato paste. Return beef to pan and bring to boil; reduce heat, cover and simmer until cabbage is tender, 15 minutes.

Stir in rice; cook until heated through, about 2 minutes. Discard bay leaves. Serve with lemon.

Makes 4 to 6 servings. PER EACH OF 6 SERVINGS: about 204 cal, 14 g pro, 8 g total fat (2 g sat. fat), 18 g carb, 3 g fibre, 31 mg chol, 588 mg sodium. % RDI: 4% calcium, 14% iron, 45% vit A, 18% vit C, 8% folate.

Waughburgers

These everything-but-the-kitchen-sink burgers are a childhood favourite of *Canadian Living* food director Annabelle Waugh. Their juicy richness comes from the mix of all sorts of condiments you likely already have in the fridge.

2 **eggs**

½ cup **dry bread crumbs**

3 tbsp minced or grated **sweet onion**

2 tbsp **wine vinegar**

2 tsp **garlic powder**

1 tsp **Worcestershire sauce**

½ tsp each **salt** and **pepper**

¼ cup **ketchup**

3 tbsp **brown steak sauce** (such as HP Sauce)

2 tbsp **Dijon mustard** or grainy mustard

4 tsp **prepared hot horseradish**

2 lb (900 g) **lean ground beef**

8 **hamburger buns,** split and toasted

In large bowl, whisk together eggs, bread crumbs, onion, vinegar, garlic powder, Worcestershire sauce, salt and pepper.

Mix together ketchup, steak sauce, mustard and horseradish; remove half and set aside. Add remaining ketchup mixture to egg mixture; mix in beef.

Shape into eight ¾-inch (2 cm) thick patties. *(Make-ahead: Layer between waxed paper in airtight container and refrigerate for up to 24 hours.)*

Place on greased grill over medium-high heat; close lid and grill, turning once and brushing occasionally with reserved sauce, until instant-read thermometer inserted sideways into centre reads 160°F (71°C), 10 to 12 minutes. Sandwich in buns.

Makes 8 servings. PER SERVING: about 392 cal, 29 g pro, 15 g total fat (5 g sat. fat), 35 g carb, 2 g fibre, 106 mg chol, 715 mg sodium, 394 mg potassium. % RDI: 10% calcium, 31% iron, 2% vit A, 3% vit C, 36% folate.

Southwestern Sloppy Joes

This Southwest-spiced version of the deliciously messy supper sandwich is a hit with adults and kids alike. If you enjoy a little heat, add an extra jalapeño pepper.

1 tbsp **olive oil**

1 **onion,** diced

1 **jalapeño pepper,** seeded and diced

2 cloves **garlic,** minced

1 lb (450 g) **lean ground beef**

2 tsp **chili powder**

1½ tsp each **ground cumin** and **ground coriander**

Pinch **salt**

1 cup **bottled strained tomatoes** (passata)

1 cup rinsed drained canned **black beans**

½ cup **frozen corn kernels**

2 tbsp **lime juice**

2 tsp **liquid honey**

2 **green onions,** chopped

4 **whole grain hamburger buns,** toasted

¾ cup shredded **Monterey Jack cheese**

In large skillet, heat oil over medium heat; cook onion, jalapeño pepper and garlic, stirring occasionally, until softened, 6 to 8 minutes.

Add beef; cook over medium-high heat, breaking up with spoon, until browned, about 5 minutes.

Drain fat from pan; cook chili powder, cumin, coriander and salt for 1 minute. Add tomatoes, beans, corn, lime juice and honey; cook until slightly thickened, 4 to 5 minutes. Stir in green onions.

Spoon evenly over bottoms of buns; sprinkle with cheese. Cover with tops of buns.

Makes 4 servings. PER SERVING: about 577 cal, 36 g pro, 28 g total fat (11 g sat. fat), 49 g carb, 9 g fibre, 82 mg chol, 715 mg sodium, 858 mg potassium. % RDI: 25% calcium, 46% iron, 9% vit A, 12% vit C, 30% folate.

KIDS LOVE IT!

Rosemary Beef Burgers With Jalapeño Mayonnaise

Fresh rosemary gives these tasty grilled patties a nice herbal note. Make a double batch of the spicy jalapeño mayo and use it to add zip to your favourite sandwiches.

1 **egg**

¼ cup **sodium-reduced beef broth**

1 small **onion,** grated

¼ cup **dry bread crumbs**

2 tsp finely chopped **fresh rosemary**

½ tsp each **salt** and **pepper**

1 lb (450 g) **lean ground beef**

4 **kaiser rolls** or hamburger buns

JALAPEÑO MAYONNAISE:

¼ cup **light mayonnaise**

2 tbsp chopped **fresh parsley**

1 tbsp minced **jalapeño pepper**

1 clove **garlic,** minced

In bowl, beat egg with broth. Stir in onion, bread crumbs, rosemary, salt and pepper; mix in beef. Shape into four ½-inch (1 cm) thick patties.

Place on greased grill over medium-high heat; close lid and grill, turning once, until instant-read thermometer inserted sideways into centre reads 160°F (71°C), about 10 minutes.

JALAPEÑO MAYONNAISE: Meanwhile, stir together mayonnaise, parsley, jalapeño pepper and garlic.

Cut rolls in half; toast, cut sides down, on grill until golden, 1 to 2 minutes. Spread jalapeño mayonnaise on cut sides. Sandwich burgers in rolls.

Makes 4 servings. PER SERVING: about 534 cal, 30 g pro, 27 g total fat (9 g sat. fat), 41 g carb, 2 g fibre, 130 mg chol, 897 mg sodium, 419 mg potassium. % RDI: 10% calcium, 32% iron, 4% vit A, 8% vit C, 39% folate.

Aromatic Beef Kabobs With Cucumber Yogurt

Also known as koftas, these ground-meat skewers are a staple of Middle Eastern street cuisine. Here they make a delicious, hearty sandwich filling.

1 lb (450 g) **lean ground beef** or lamb

¼ cup **dried currants** or chopped raisins

¼ cup **dry bread crumbs**

2 tbsp minced **fresh cilantro**

1 tbsp each minced **fresh ginger** and **garlic**

½ tsp each **cinnamon, pepper, dried oregano** and **dried thyme**

¼ tsp each **salt** and **ground cumin**

4 **Greek-style pita breads** (pocketless)

2 cups shredded **red leaf lettuce** or romaine lettuce

CUCUMBER YOGURT:

1 cup **Balkan-style plain yogurt**

½ cup grated peeled **cucumber**

1 **green onion,** thinly sliced

1 tsp **lemon juice**

½ tsp each **salt** and **granulated sugar**

CUCUMBER YOGURT: Stir together yogurt, cucumber, green onion, lemon juice, salt and sugar. Set aside in refrigerator.

Mix together beef, currants, bread crumbs, cilantro, ginger, garlic, cinnamon, pepper, oregano, thyme, salt and cumin. Divide into 12 portions; form into egg shapes, flattening slightly. Thread onto skewers.

Place on greased grill over medium-high heat; close lid and grill, turning twice, until instant-read thermometer inserted into centre of several reads 160°F (71°C), about 10 minutes.

Meanwhile, grill pitas on both sides until slightly crisp, about 2 minutes. Serve kabobs, lettuce and cucumber yogurt in pitas.

Makes 4 servings. PER SERVING: about 518 cal, 31 g pro, 18 g total fat (8 g sat. fat), 53 g carb, 3 g fibre, 73 mg chol, 904 mg sodium. % RDI: 18% calcium, 36% iron, 9% vit A, 7% vit C, 31% folate.

Giant Meatballs in Tomato Fennel Sauce

Sure to be a big hit with kids, these great-big meatballs have fabulous flavour and taste even better the next day. You might want to make a double batch and freeze half for later. Serve over your favourite long pasta.

2 cups cubed crustless **Italian bread**

1 cup **milk**

1 each **egg** and **egg yolk**

1 lb (450 g) **ground beef** or ground veal

1 lb (450 g) **ground pork**

2 tbsp **olive oil**

3 cloves **garlic,** minced

½ cup minced **shallots** or onion

¼ cup chopped **fresh parsley**

¼ cup grated **Parmesan cheese**

¼ tsp each **salt** and **pepper**

3 tbsp **all-purpose flour**

TOMATO FENNEL SAUCE:

2 tbsp **olive oil**

1 **onion,** chopped

4 cloves **garlic,** sliced

Half **fennel bulb,** cored and chopped

1 small **carrot,** chopped

½ tsp **salt**

¼ tsp **hot pepper flakes**

1 can (28 oz/796 mL) **whole tomatoes**

10 **fresh basil leaves** (or fresh parsley sprigs)

TOMATO FENNEL SAUCE: In Dutch oven, heat oil over medium heat; cook onion, garlic, fennel, carrot, salt and hot pepper flakes, stirring occasionally, until softened, about 8 minutes. Add tomatoes, breaking up with spoon. Stir in 1 cup water and basil; bring to boil. Reduce heat, cover and simmer for 30 minutes. Let cool slightly. Transfer to food processor; blend until smooth. Return to clean Dutch oven.

Meanwhile, in bowl, soak cubed bread in milk until absorbed, about 10 minutes. Squeeze out as much of the milk as possible.

In food processor, pulse together bread mixture, egg, egg yolk and about one-quarter each of the beef and pork just until incorporated. Transfer to large bowl.

Meanwhile, in skillet, heat 1 tbsp of the oil over medium-low heat; cook garlic and shallots until golden, 3 to 5 minutes. Add to bread mixture along with parsley, Parmesan cheese, salt, pepper and remaining veal and pork; mix with hands just until combined. Form into 12 large meatballs; refrigerate for 10 minutes. Gently roll in flour.

In large skillet, heat remaining oil over medium-high heat; cook meatballs until browned all over, about 8 minutes. Add to sauce; cover and simmer over medium-low heat, stirring and basting occasionally, until instant-read thermometer inserted into several reads 160°F (71°C), about 20 minutes.

Makes 6 to 8 servings. PER EACH OF 8 SERVINGS: about 415 cal, 27 g pro, 26 g total fat (9 g sat. fat), 17 g carb, 2 g fibre, 124 mg chol, 540 mg sodium, 723 mg potassium. % RDI: 12% calcium, 26% iron, 20% vit A, 32% vit C, 23% folate.

SAVE
SOME FOR
LUNCH

ONE-POT WONDER

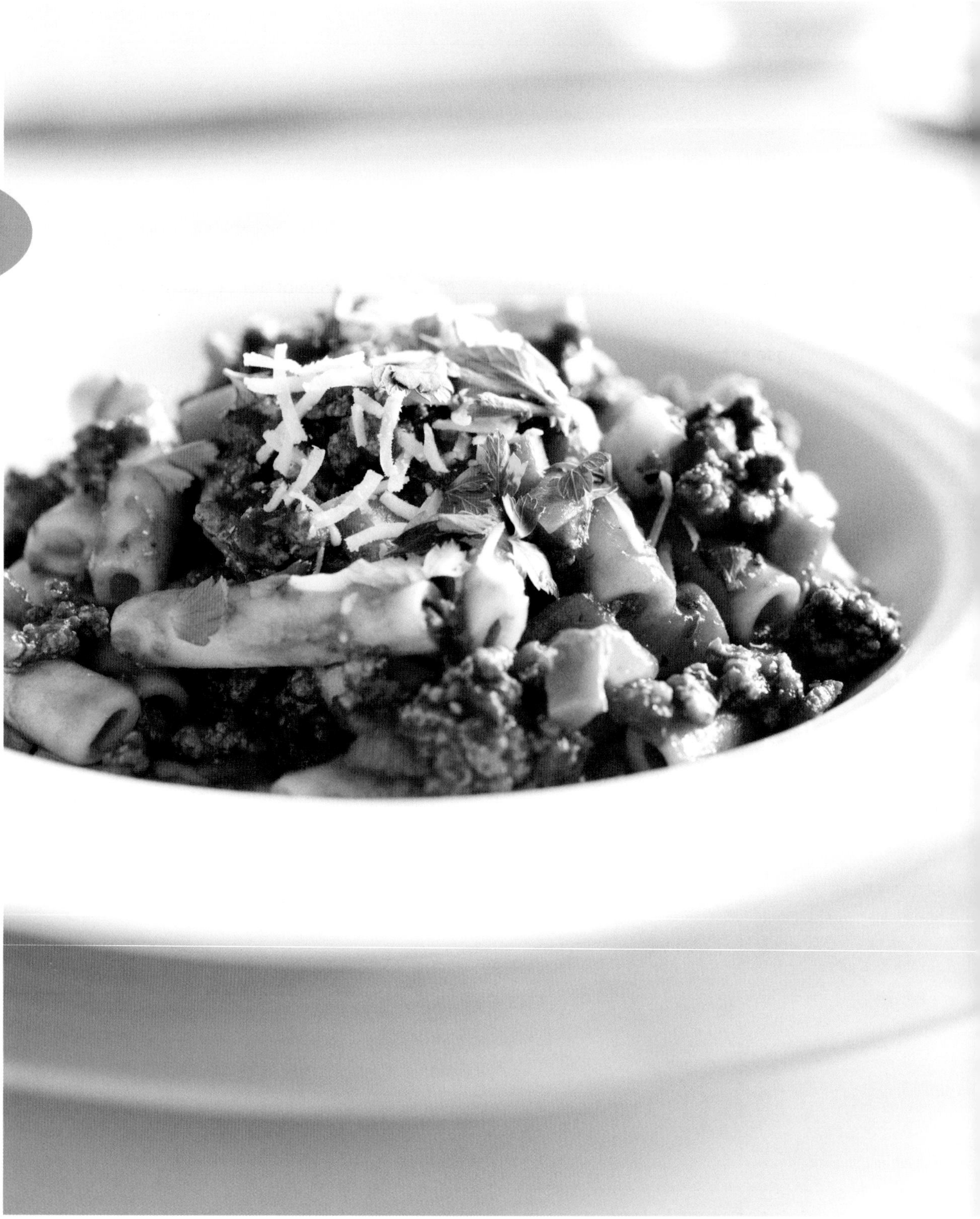

Ziti With Beef Sauce

Ziti and other large tube-style pastas are the ideal shape for hanging on to this chunky sauce. Sprinkle with more Parmesan or parsley at the table.

2 cups **ziti pasta** or penne pasta

1 lb (450 g) **lean ground beef**

1 tbsp **extra-virgin olive oil**

1 each rib **celery** and **carrot,** diced

1 small **onion,** diced

1 thick slice **bacon,** diced

2 cloves **garlic,** minced

1 tsp **dried oregano**

¼ tsp each **salt** and **pepper**

Pinch **hot pepper flakes**

3 tbsp **tomato paste**

1 can (28 oz/796 mL) **diced tomatoes**

1 tbsp **balsamic vinegar**

¾ cup grated **Parmesan cheese**

¼ cup minced **fresh parsley**

In large saucepan of boiling salted water, cook pasta until al dente, about 8 minutes. Drain and set aside.

In same saucepan, sauté beef over medium-high heat, breaking up with spoon, until no longer pink, about 5 minutes. Using slotted spoon, transfer beef to bowl; set aside.

Drain fat from pan. Heat oil over medium-high heat; sauté celery, carrot, onion, bacon, garlic, oregano, salt, pepper and hot pepper flakes until vegetables are softened, about 5 minutes.

Stir in tomato paste; cook for 1 minute. Return beef to pan. Add tomatoes and vinegar; simmer, stirring often, until thickened and vegetables are tender, about 15 minutes.

Add pasta to pan. Add Parmesan cheese and parsley; cook until heated through, 2 minutes.

Makes 4 servings. PER SERVING: about 596 cal, 38 g pro, 28 g total fat (12 g sat. fat), 47 g carb, 5 g fibre, 86 mg chol, 958 mg sodium. % RDI: 29% calcium, 49% iron, 42% vit A, 60% vit C, 50% folate.

Slow Cooker Braised Beef & Rosemary Pasta Sauce

A splash of balsamic vinegar adds polish to this rich beef-based sauce.

1½ lb (675 g) **stewing beef cubes**

1 tbsp **vegetable oil**

1 small **onion,** chopped

1 tbsp **dried rosemary**

½ tsp each **salt** and **pepper**

1 can (28 oz/796 mL) **stewed tomatoes**

2 tbsp **balsamic vinegar** or red wine vinegar

¼ cup grated **Parmesan cheese**

Trim and cut beef into 1-inch (2.5 cm) cubes. In large skillet, heat oil over medium-high heat; brown beef, in batches. Using slotted spoon, transfer to slow cooker.

Drain fat from skillet. Cook onion, rosemary, salt and pepper over medium-low heat, stirring occasionally, until softened, about 4 minutes. Add to slow cooker.

Add ¼ cup water to skillet; bring to boil, scraping up browned bits. Add to slow cooker along with tomatoes and vinegar.

Cover and cook on high until beef is tender, 4 to 6 hours (or cook on low for 8 to 10 hours). Serve sprinkled with Parmesan cheese.

make it a meal!

Just Add Pasta

Boil your favourite short pasta to go with this sauce – you'll need about 3 cups to make six servings. Just follow the package directions and cook until al dente.

Makes 6 servings. PER SERVING: about 258 cal, 28 g pro, 12 g total fat (4 g sat. fat), 9 g carb, 2 g fibre, 59 mg chol, 557 mg sodium. % RDI: 10% calcium, 24% iron, 9% vit A, 22% vit C, 7% folate.

Saucy Beef Simmer

Like many stews, this one contains tender beef and onion, but it's enhanced by a touch of Greek spicing: oregano and the subtle, homey flavour of cinnamon.

1½ lb (675 g) **stewing beef cubes**

½ tsp each **salt** and **pepper**

2 tbsp **vegetable oil**

2 ribs **celery,** chopped

1 **onion,** chopped

4 cloves **garlic,** minced

½ tsp **dried oregano**

¼ tsp **cinnamon**

¼ cup **all-purpose flour**

2 cups **beef broth**

⅓ cup **tomato paste**

¼ cup chopped **fresh parsley**

Trim and cut beef into 1-inch (2.5 cm) cubes; sprinkle with salt and pepper. In large saucepan, heat half of the oil over medium-high heat; brown beef, in batches. Transfer to plate.

Drain any fat from pan; add remaining oil. Fry celery, onion, garlic, oregano and cinnamon over medium heat, stirring occasionally, until onion is softened, about 5 minutes.

Stir in flour; cook for 1 minute. Stir in broth, 1 cup water and tomato paste, scraping up any browned bits. Return beef and any accumulated juices to pan; bring to boil. Reduce heat, cover and simmer, stirring occasionally, until beef is tender, about 1½ hours. Serve sprinkled with parsley.

Makes 4 to 6 servings. PER EACH OF 6 SERVINGS: about 270 cal, 28 g pro, 13 g total fat (4 g sat. fat), 10 g carb, 1 g fibre, 55 mg chol, 542 mg sodium. % RDI: 3% calcium, 25% iron, 5% vit A, 20% vit C, 12% folate.

Budget-Friendly Red Meat

What Makes It Affordable: Less-tender cuts of meat – the ones labelled "stewing" or "marinating" in your supermarket – have always been a bargain, relative to more-tender grilling steaks or oven roasts. So have ground beef and lamb, which are made from small pieces that would otherwise be wasted. Lean and extra-lean ground beef tend to be a little more expensive than medium or regular, but they are lower in saturated fat and calories (they also yield more lean meat, because less fat renders out of them). Ground lamb tends to be on the fatty side, but gives rich flavour to kabobs and koftas.

Lamb shoulder is typically the least expensive of the larger cuts of lamb (chops, steaks and oven roasts tend to be quite pricey). It's fattier and suited to braising in stews and curries, in which a small amount of meat stretches a long way.

Why It's Good for You: Beef and lamb are both excellent sources of protein, vitamin B_{12}, niacin and zinc. They're also sources of iron. Beef is a source of riboflavin, while lamb is an excellent source of this vitamin.

Food Safety: Like all meats, beef and lamb need to be handled properly to keep you safe from illness. Cook them to the proper temperature to ensure all bacteria are killed. It's especially important to cook ground meats well – until an instant-read thermometer reads 160°F (71°C) – because they have more surface area for bacteria to hide on.

Always use a clean plate for cooked meat (never the same one the raw meat was on) and chill any leftovers within two hours of cooking. If you buy meat on sale and freeze it for later, thaw it on a plate to catch the juices – always in the refrigerator, not at room temperature. It's best to allow at least a day for small cuts to thaw; roasts can take up to a couple of days in the fridge.

Uses: It's easy to transform chewier cuts – such as beef round steaks and roasts, flank steaks, cross-rib pot roasts or lamb shoulder roasts – into juicy, fall-apart-tender ones if you cook them in a way that maximizes tenderness. Braising, stewing, pot-roasting or any long, slow, moist cooking method will yield fork-tender results. Ground beef and lamb are wonderful in all manner of dishes, from burgers to curries to chilis.

Creamy Beef Noodles

This dish is made with ingredients most people keep in their refrigerators and pantries. Evaporated milk makes the sauce deliciously creamy without all the added fat of whipping cream.

1 tbsp **butter**

1 **onion,** finely chopped

2 cloves **garlic,** minced

12 oz (340 g) **lean ground beef**

⅓ cup **all-purpose flour**

1 cup **sodium-reduced beef broth**

1 can (370 mL) **evaporated milk**

1 cup **frozen peas**

1 cup shredded **extra-old Cheddar cheese**

⅓ cup chopped **fresh parsley**

4 tsp **Dijon mustard**

¼ tsp each **salt** and **pepper**

1¾ cups **elbow macaroni**

In Dutch oven or large saucepan, melt butter over medium-high heat; cook onion, stirring occasionally, until beginning to soften, about 2 minutes. Add garlic; cook for 1 minute.

Add beef; cook, breaking up with spoon, until browned, about 4 minutes. Stir in flour; cook, stirring, for 2 minutes.

Stir in broth and milk; bring to boil. Reduce heat to medium; stir in peas, Cheddar cheese, parsley, mustard, salt and pepper.

Meanwhile, in pot of boiling salted water, cook pasta until al dente. Reserving ⅓ cup of the cooking liquid, drain. Add pasta to sauce, tossing to coat and adding enough of the reserved cooking liquid so that sauce coats noodles.

Makes 4 servings. PER SERVING: about 663 cal, 41 g pro, 27 g total fat (14 g sat. fat), 62 g carb, 5 g fibre, 96 mg chol, 897 mg sodium, 737 mg potassium. % RDI: 48% calcium, 36% iron, 27% vit A, 72% vit C, 73% folate.

PANTRY
SUPERSTAR

Skillet Beef & Corn Pie

Just like *pastel de choclo,* a popular Chilean dish, this pie is loaded with raisins, olives and hard-cooked eggs. Serve with fresh tomato salsa or a squeeze of lime.

1 tbsp **vegetable oil**

1½ lb (675 g) **extra-lean ground beef**

2 **onions,** chopped

2 cloves **garlic,** minced

1 tbsp **chili powder**

1 tsp **ground cumin**

¼ tsp each **salt** and **pepper**

3 tbsp **all-purpose flour**

1½ cups **sodium-reduced beef broth**

1 cup **frozen corn kernels,** thawed

½ cup **dark raisins**

⅓ cup **Kalamata olives,** halved and pitted

2 **hard-cooked eggs** (see How-To, page 237), quartered

CORN TOPPING:

1 cup **frozen corn kernels,** thawed

½ cup **buttermilk**

1 **egg**

3 tbsp **unsalted butter,** melted

⅔ cup each **cornmeal** and **all-purpose flour**

1½ tsp **baking powder**

½ tsp **baking soda**

¼ tsp **salt**

In deep 10-inch (25 cm) ovenproof cast-iron or nonstick skillet, heat oil over medium-high heat; cook beef, breaking up with spoon, until browned, about 2 minutes. Add onions; cook, stirring often, until softened, about 6 minutes.

Add garlic, chili powder, cumin, salt and pepper; cook, stirring, for 3 minutes.

Reduce heat to medium. Stir in flour until absorbed. Stir in broth, scraping up browned bits; cook, stirring occasionally, until thickened, 3 to 5 minutes. Stir in corn, raisins and olives; remove from heat. Nestle eggs in beef mixture; set aside.

CORN TOPPING: In food processor, purée corn until almost smooth, about 1 minute. Add buttermilk, egg and butter; blend until combined. Transfer to bowl. Whisk together cornmeal, flour, baking powder, baking soda and salt; stir into corn mixture just until combined. Spoon evenly over beef mixture, leaving ½-inch (1 cm) border around edge for steam to escape.

Bake in 400°F (200°C) oven until topping is golden, 20 to 25 minutes. Let stand for 5 minutes before serving.

Makes 6 servings. PER SERVING: about 549 cal, 34 g pro, 23 g total fat (9 g sat. fat), 53 g carb, 4 g fibre, 182 mg chol, 777 mg sodium, 748 mg potassium. % RDI: 11% calcium, 33% iron, 15% vit A, 7% vit C, 45% folate.

Mince & Tatties

The original Scottish comfort food, this simple supper is wonderful on a cool night when you need a filling all-in-one dish to warm you up.

1 lb (450 g) **lean ground beef**

1 large **onion,** diced

¼ cup **butter**

¼ cup **all-purpose flour**

3 cups **Meat Stock** (page 241) or sodium-reduced beef broth

2 **carrots,** diced

1 tsp **Worcestershire sauce**

¾ tsp each **salt** and **pepper**

Pinch **ground cloves**

1 cup **frozen peas**

6 **yellow-fleshed potatoes** (unpeeled), cut in half

¾ cup **warm milk**

In saucepan, cook beef over medium-high heat, breaking up with spoon, for 5 minutes. Add onion; cook, stirring occasionally, until beef is browned and onions are golden, about 7 minutes.

Add ¼ cup water and 2 tbsp of the butter; cook, scraping up browned bits, until butter is melted and no liquid remains. Stir in flour; cook, stirring, for 2 minutes. Gradually stir in stock; bring to boil. Reduce heat and simmer, stirring occasionally, until thickened and liquid is reduced slightly, about 20 minutes.

Add carrots, Worcestershire sauce, ¼ tsp each of the salt and pepper, and cloves; simmer, stirring occasionally, until carrots are tender, about 10 minutes. Stir in peas; cook until heated through, about 2 minutes.

Meanwhile, in large saucepan of boiling salted water, cook potatoes until tender, 25 minutes. Drain and return to pan; mash in milk and remaining butter, salt and pepper. Serve topped with meat mixture.

Makes 4 servings. PER SERVING: about 694 cal, 36 g pro, 29 g total fat (14 g sat. fat), 75 g carb, 8 g fibre, 102 mg chol, 1,651 mg sodium, 1,924 mg potassium. % RDI: 13% calcium, 43% iron, 82% vit A, 63% vit C, 38% folate.

SIMPLER
& EASIER

Beef & Black Bean Enchilada Bake

Making enchiladas usually involves rolling tortillas around a savoury filling. But for this tasty recipe, there's no rolling involved – just layer, bake and enjoy!

2 cups **bottled strained tomatoes** (passata)

2 cloves **garlic,** minced

2 tbsp **chili powder**

1 tsp **dried oregano**

1 **canned chipotle pepper in adobo sauce,** chopped

Pinch **salt**

1 lb (450 g) **lean ground beef**

2 tsp **olive oil**

1 **onion,** finely chopped

1 cup rinsed drained **canned black beans**

¾ cup **frozen corn kernels**

3 large **whole wheat tortillas**

1¼ cups shredded **Cheddar cheese**

¼ cup **sour cream**

1 **green onion,** thinly sliced

In small saucepan, bring strained tomatoes, garlic, chili powder, oregano, chipotle pepper and salt to boil; reduce heat and simmer for 10 minutes.

Meanwhile, in large nonstick skillet, cook beef over medium-high heat, breaking up with spoon, until browned. Using slotted spoon, remove beef and set aside.

Drain fat from pan; add oil. Cook onion, stirring occasionally, over medium heat until softened, 3 to 4 minutes. Add black beans and corn. Return beef to pan, stirring to combine. Stir in 1 cup of the sauce, mixing well.

Place 1 of the tortillas in greased 8-inch (2 L) square baking dish; top with ¼ cup of the cheese and half of the meat mixture. Repeat layers once. Top with remaining tortilla and sauce. Sprinkle with remaining cheese.

Bake in 375°F (190°C) oven until cheese is melted, about 15 minutes. Slice and serve garnished with sour cream and green onion.

Makes 4 servings. PER SERVING: about 650 cal, 40 g pro, 33 g total fat (15 g sat. fat), 47 g carb, 8 g fibre, 104 mg chol, 1,094 mg sodium, 898 mg potassium. % RDI: 32% calcium, 51% iron, 25% vit A, 13% vit C, 35% folate.

Cheddar Cottage Pie

Cottage pie is the beef-based equivalent of shepherd's pie, which traditionally contains lamb or mutton. This flavourful one is comforting and cheesy – perfect for family dinners.

1 tbsp **vegetable oil**

1 **onion,** diced

2 large **carrots,** diced

2 cloves **garlic,** minced

1 lb (450 g) **lean ground beef**

½ tsp **dried thyme**

¼ tsp each **salt** and **pepper**

2 tbsp **tomato paste**

1⅓ cups **sodium-reduced beef broth**

1 tbsp **Worcestershire sauce**

CHEDDAR MASHED POTATOES:

2 lb (900 g) **baking potatoes** (4 or 5), peeled

1 cup **milk**

1 cup shredded **extra-old Cheddar cheese**

CHEDDAR MASHED POTATOES: In large saucepan of boiling salted water, cook potatoes until tender, about 10 minutes. Drain and set aside. In same saucepan, heat milk until bubbles form around edge; remove from heat. Add potatoes; mash with potato masher. Beat with electric beater until smooth. Stir in cheese.

Meanwhile, in large skillet, heat oil over medium heat; cook onion, carrots and garlic, stirring occasionally, until softened, about 5 minutes. Add beef, thyme, salt and pepper; cook, stirring, until beef is no longer pink. Stir in tomato paste.

Stir in broth and Worcestershire sauce; bring to boil. Cover, reduce heat and simmer over medium heat for 15 minutes.

Pour meat mixture into 6-cup (1.5 L) casserole dish. Spread mashed potatoes evenly over top. Bake in 400°F (200°C) oven until bubbly and browned, about 20 minutes.

know your ingredients

Boiling vs. Baking Potatoes

Boiling potatoes, such as white potatoes, have a waxy texture, which helps them hold their shape when boiled. Baking potatoes, such as russet potatoes, have a floury, or fluffy, texture that makes them better for baking, mashing and frying. All-purpose yellow-fleshed potatoes, commonly found in grocery stores, can typically be substituted for either category.

Makes 4 to 6 servings. PER EACH OF 6 SERVINGS: about 407 cal, 24 g pro, 20 g total fat (9 g sat. fat), 33 g carb, 3 g fibre, 68 mg chol, 470 mg sodium, 864 mg potassium. % RDI: 21% calcium, 18% iron, 61% vit A, 20% vit C, 13% folate.

Meat Loaf With Glazed Vegetables

Meat loaf is popular because it's quick and easy to toss together, hearty and always delicious – especially when covered with a glossy vegetable topping.

1 tbsp **olive oil**

1 **red onion,** diced

1 **carrot,** diced

1 small **eggplant,** diced

1 **zucchini,** diced

1 **sweet red pepper,** diced

3 cloves **garlic,** minced

1 cup **bottled strained tomatoes** (passata)

¼ cup **red wine vinegar**

1½ lb (675 g) **extra-lean ground beef**

2 **eggs**

½ cup chopped **fresh parsley**

½ cup **large-flake rolled oats**

¼ cup **milk**

¾ tsp **salt**

½ tsp **pepper**

In skillet, heat oil over medium heat; cook onion, carrot and eggplant, stirring occasionally, until onion is softened, about 8 minutes.

Add zucchini, red pepper and garlic; cook until tender, about 6 minutes. Stir in tomatoes and 2 tbsp of the vinegar. Set aside.

In large bowl, mix together beef, eggs, parsley, rolled oats, milk, salt, pepper, remaining vinegar and half of the vegetable mixture. Press into 9- x 5-inch (2 L) loaf pan; spread remaining vegetable mixture over top.

Bake in 350°F (180°C) oven until instant-read thermometer inserted into centre reads 160°F (71°C), about 1¼ hours. Tent with foil and let stand for 10 minutes before slicing.

Makes 8 servings. PER SERVING: about 246 cal, 22 g pro, 10 g total fat (4 g sat. fat), 16 g carb, 3 g fibre, 94 mg chol, 358 mg sodium, 582 mg potassium. % RDI: 5% calcium, 24% iron, 29% vit A, 53% vit C, 16% folate.

Harissa Meat Loaf With Coriander Mash

Look for fiery harissa paste in Middle Eastern stores and some supermarkets.

2 tsp **olive oil**

1 **onion,** finely chopped

1 tbsp **harissa**

3 cloves **garlic,** minced

1 tsp **ground coriander**

¼ tsp **cinnamon**

½ cup **dried figs,** finely chopped

3 tbsp **couscous** (or ½ cup fresh bread crumbs)

1 **egg**

1 lb (450 g) **lean ground beef**

CORIANDER MASH:

2 lb (900 g) **yellow-fleshed potatoes** (about 4 large), peeled and chopped

¼ cup **butter**

1 **onion,** thinly sliced

1 tsp **ground coriander**

¾ tsp **salt**

½ tsp **pepper**

TOMATO HARISSA SAUCE:

1 cup **bottled strained tomatoes** (passata)

1 tbsp each **liquid honey** and **white wine vinegar**

2 tsp **harissa**

1 clove **garlic,** minced

Pinch **salt**

In large skillet, heat oil over medium heat; cook onion, stirring occasionally, until softened, about 5 minutes. Stir in harissa, garlic, coriander and cinnamon; cook, stirring, for 1 minute. Scrape into large bowl; let cool.

Add figs, couscous and egg to onion mixture; stir in beef until combined. Press into 8- x 4-inch (1.5 L) loaf pan, rounding top. Bake in 350°F (180°C) oven until instant-read thermometer inserted into centre reads 160°F (71°C), 35 to 45 minutes. Let stand for 5 minutes before slicing.

CORIANDER MASH: In large pot of boiling lightly salted water, cook potatoes until tender, about 15 minutes. Reserving 1 cup of the cooking liquid, drain and mash potatoes. Meanwhile, in small saucepan, melt butter over medium heat; cook onion, coriander, salt and pepper, stirring often, until onion is light golden, about 8 minutes. Stir into potatoes along with enough of the reserved cooking liquid to loosen to desired consistency.

TOMATO HARISSA SAUCE: In saucepan, combine tomatoes, honey, vinegar, harissa, garlic and salt; bring to boil. Reduce heat to medium; simmer, stirring occasionally, until reduced to ¾ cup, 10 to 15 minutes. Serve with meat loaf and potatoes.

Makes 6 servings. PER SERVING: about 473 cal, 20 g pro, 23 g total fat (10 g sat. fat), 48 g carb, 5 g fibre, 97 mg chol, 814 mg sodium, 921 mg potassium. % RDI: 6% calcium, 25% iron, 12% vit A, 20% vit C, 14% folate.

Salsa-Stuffed Muffin Meat Loaves

Black beans add fibre to the tasty beef mixture and perfectly match the Tex-Mex seasonings in these pint-size loaves. Add the remaining canned black beans to your lunchtime salad or tomorrow's chili.

½ cup **fresh whole wheat bread crumbs**

1 **green onion,** chopped

½ cup rinsed drained **canned black beans**

1½ tsp **chili powder**

½ tsp **pepper**

Pinch **salt**

1 **egg**

1 lb (450 g) **extra-lean ground beef**

⅓ cup **salsa**

½ cup shredded **Monterey Jack cheese** or Cheddar cheese

In large bowl, combine bread crumbs, green onion, black beans, chili powder, pepper, salt and egg; mix in beef. Shape into 8 balls. Place each in lightly greased muffin cup.

With spoon, make indentation in centre of each; fill with salsa and sprinkle with cheese.

Bake in 400°F (200°C) oven until instant-read thermometer inserted into centre of several reads 160°F (71°C), about 15 minutes.

Makes 4 servings. PER SERVING: about 335 cal, 32 g pro, 15 g total fat (7 g sat. fat), 16 g carb, 4 g fibre, 122 mg chol, 482 mg sodium, 543 mg potassium. % RDI: 15% calcium, 28% iron, 8% vit A, 3% vit C, 19% folate.

Beef Patties With Saucy Mushrooms

These burgers-sans-buns have a rich yet simple mushroom topping that makes them a lot dressier than the usual weeknight supper.

1 **onion**

1 **egg**

2 tbsp **dry bread crumbs**

¾ tsp **dried thyme**

½ tsp each **salt** and **pepper**

3 cloves **garlic,** minced

1 lb (450 g) **lean ground beef**

1 tbsp **vegetable oil**

2½ cups sliced **mushrooms**

2 tbsp **all-purpose flour**

1½ cups **sodium-reduced chicken broth**

½ tsp **Worcestershire sauce**

2 tsp chopped **fresh parsley**

Grate half of the onion. Slice remaining half and set aside.

In large bowl, combine grated onion, egg, bread crumbs, 1 tbsp water, thyme, salt, pepper and half of the garlic; mix in beef. Shape into eight ½-inch (1 cm) thick patties.

In large skillet, heat oil over medium heat; fry patties, turning once, until instant-read thermometer inserted sideways into centre reads 160°F (71°C), about 10 minutes. Transfer to plate.

Drain fat from pan. Fry mushrooms, sliced onion and remaining garlic until mushrooms are softened and browned, about 4 minutes. Add flour; cook, stirring, for 1 minute. Add broth and Worcestershire sauce; bring to boil. Boil, stirring, until thickened, about 2 minutes. Return patties to pan and sprinkle with parsley; cook until heated through.

Makes 4 servings. PER SERVING: about 297 cal, 25 g pro, 17 g total fat (5 g sat. fat), 11 g carb, 1 g fibre, 108 mg chol, 676 mg sodium. % RDI: 4% calcium, 25% iron, 2% vit A, 7% vit C, 14% folate.

QUICK
PREP

Quick Beef Bulgogi

Bulgogi, a Korean marinated beef dish, is traditionally served with rice and spicy kimchi pickles. Use whatever grilling steak is on sale – a single pound (450 g) is plenty to feed four people. If you can't find Asian pears, use any firm pear.

3 tbsp **sodium-reduced soy sauce**

2 tbsp **mirin** or white wine

1 tbsp each **granulated sugar** and **sesame seeds**

1 tbsp **sesame oil**

3 cloves **garlic,** minced

2 tsp minced **fresh ginger**

4 **green onions,** thinly sliced

Half **Asian pear,** peeled and grated (about ⅓ cup)

1 lb (450 g) **beef grilling steak,** thinly sliced

1 tsp **vegetable oil**

In bowl, whisk together soy sauce, mirin, sugar, sesame seeds, sesame oil, garlic, ginger and all but 2 tbsp of the green onions until sugar is dissolved.

Stir in pear and beef; cover and let stand for 15 minutes or refrigerate for up to 2 hours. Drain off marinade.

In wok or skillet, heat vegetable oil over high heat; stir-fry beef mixture until beef is browned, about 3 minutes. Garnish with remaining green onions.

Makes 4 servings. PER SERVING: about 204 cal, 24 g pro, 9 g total fat (3 g sat. fat), 6 g carb, 1 g fibre, 53 mg chol, 293 mg sodium, 361 mg potassium. % RDI: 2% calcium, 19% iron, 1% vit A, 3% vit C, 6% folate.

Black Bean Beef & Asparagus

In many Chinese dishes, meat is a flavouring, not the focus. Here, ground beef adds texture and rich flavour to a mix of tender noodles and asparagus.

6 **green onions**

1 lb (450 g) **asparagus,** trimmed

1 lb (450 g) **lean ground beef**

2 tbsp **vegetable oil**

3 cloves **garlic,** minced

2 tsp grated **fresh ginger**

1 **Thai bird's-eye pepper,** minced (optional)

2 tbsp **black bean sauce**

12 oz (340 g) **Chinese wheat noodles** or linguine

⅓ cup **sodium-reduced chicken broth**

2 tbsp **dry sherry** (optional)

1 tbsp **sodium-reduced soy sauce**

2 tsp each **granulated sugar** and **cornstarch**

Half **English cucumber,** cut in 2-inch (5 cm) sticks

Cut green onions into white and green parts. Mince white parts. Cut 3 of the green parts into 2-inch (5 cm) lengths. Set aside.

In saucepan of boiling water, blanch asparagus until tender-crisp, 3 to 5 minutes; cut into 2-inch (5 cm) lengths. Place beef in colander; submerge in boiling water for 1 minute. Drain.

In wok or large skillet, heat oil over medium-high heat; stir-fry garlic, white parts of green onions, ginger, Thai pepper (if using) and beef until fragrant and no liquid remains, about 5 minutes. Add black bean sauce; stir-fry for 1 minute.

Meanwhile, in large saucepan of boiling water, cook noodles according to package directions. Drain; rinse and drain again. Set aside.

Whisk together broth, ½ cup water, sherry (if using), soy sauce, sugar and cornstarch; add to wok. Add asparagus and green parts of onions; cook, stirring, until thickened and glossy, and asparagus is heated through. Toss with noodles. Garnish with cucumber.

Makes 4 servings. PER SERVING: about 786 cal, 34 g pro, 39 g total fat (13 g sat. fat), 75 g carb, 8 g fibre, 155 mg chol, 613 mg sodium. % RDI: 8% calcium, 34% iron, 11% vit A, 17% vit C, 70% folate.

Ground Beef Curry

Ground beef often goes on sale, and that's the time to buy an extra pound or two to stick in the freezer for quick weeknight dinners like this mouth-watering, simple Indian curry.

3 tbsp **vegetable oil**

2 **onions,** diced

1 tbsp each minced **garlic** and **fresh ginger**

2 tbsp **Madras curry powder**

2 tbsp **tomato paste**

¾ tsp **salt**

Pinch **hot pepper flakes**

1 lb (450 g) **lean ground beef**

1 lb (450 g) **yellow-fleshed potatoes,** peeled and diced

1 can (14 oz/398 mL) **diced tomatoes**

1 tbsp **sodium-reduced soy sauce**

1 cup **frozen peas**

In large shallow Dutch oven, heat oil over medium heat; cook onions, stirring occasionally, until golden, about 12 minutes.

Add garlic and ginger; cook for 3 minutes. Add curry powder, tomato paste, salt and hot pepper flakes; cook, stirring, for 2 minutes. Add beef; cook, breaking up with spoon, until browned. Add potatoes; cook for 2 minutes.

Add tomatoes, soy sauce and 1 cup water; bring to boil. Reduce heat, cover and simmer until potatoes are tender, about 15 minutes. Stir in peas; cook for 5 minutes.

Makes 4 to 6 servings. PER EACH OF 6 SERVINGS: about 328 cal, 19 g pro, 18 g total fat (5 g sat. fat), 25 g carb, 4 g fibre, 45 mg chol, 548 mg sodium, 712 mg potassium. % RDI: 6% calcium, 24% iron, 6% vit A, 30% vit C, 16% folate.

Ground Beef & Green Bean Stir-Fry

Greens beans are a frugal backyard gardener's dream. The plants produce abundantly, and this recipe is a unique way to use up a bunch at one time.

1 lb (450 g) **green beans,** trimmed

2 tbsp **black bean sauce**

1 tbsp **cornstarch**

1 tbsp **oyster sauce**

¼ tsp **granulated sugar**

2 tbsp **vegetable oil**

12 oz (340 g) **ground beef**

1 **onion,** sliced

3 cloves **garlic,** thinly sliced

1 **green finger hot pepper**
  (or half jalapeño pepper),
  thinly sliced

¼ cup chopped **fresh cilantro**

In saucepan of boiling water, blanch green beans for 2 minutes. Drain and pat dry. Set aside.

Meanwhile, whisk together black bean sauce, cornstarch, oyster sauce and sugar; set aside.

In wok or large skillet, heat oil over high heat; stir-fry beef until no longer pink, about 4 minutes.

Add onion, garlic and hot pepper; stir-fry until onion is softened, about 3 minutes.

Add green beans and sauce mixture; stir-fry until beans are tender-crisp, about 3 minutes, adding up to 2 tbsp water to prevent sticking, if necessary. Stir in cilantro.

know your ingredients
Black Bean Sauce

Different brands of black bean sauce vary greatly in strength and saltiness. You may need to use up to ¼ cup to make a full-flavoured sauce.

Makes 4 servings. PER SERVING: about 385 cal, 17 g pro, 28 g total fat (9 g sat. fat), 17 g carb, 4 g fibre, 56 mg chol, 265 mg sodium, 415 mg potassium. % RDI: 6% calcium, 20% iron, 7% vit A, 17% vit C, 18% folate.

FRESHLY
PICKED

Pot Roast With Parsnips, Turnips & Pearl Onions

This economical cut cooks to tenderness in its own vegetable-dense gravy. It makes a large number of servings, and leftovers heat up well the next day.

2 each large **parsnips,** large **carrots** and **white turnips,** peeled

2 tbsp **all-purpose flour**

½ tsp each **salt** and **pepper**

3 lb (1.35 kg) **boneless beef pot roast** (such as top or bottom blade, or cross rib)

2 tbsp **vegetable oil**

1 large **onion,** diced

3 cloves **garlic,** sliced

1 cup **sodium-reduced beef broth**

1 can (28 oz/796 mL) **whole tomatoes,** drained

½ tsp **dried marjoram** or dried thyme

2 **bay leaves**

1 tbsp **butter**

1 pkg (10 oz/300 g) **pearl onions,** peeled

Cut parsnips and carrots in half lengthwise; cut into 2-inch (5 cm) long pieces. Quarter turnips. Set aside.

In large bowl, combine flour, salt and pepper; dredge roast in flour mixture. In Dutch oven, heat half of the oil over medium-high heat; brown roast all over. Transfer to plate.

Add remaining oil to pan; cook onion and garlic over medium heat, stirring, until softened, about 4 minutes. Add broth, scraping up any browned bits. Add tomatoes, parsnips, carrots, turnips, marjoram and bay leaves. Return beef and any accumulated juices to pan; bring to simmer. Cover and braise in 300°F (150°C) oven, basting every 30 minutes and turning once, for 2½ hours.

Meanwhile, in skillet, melt butter over medium heat; cook pearl onions until tender and golden, 10 minutes. Add to roast; cook, uncovered, until beef is tender, 30 minutes. Discard bay leaves.

Transfer roast to cutting board and tent with foil; let stand for 10 minutes before thinly slicing across the grain. Serve with vegetables and sauce.

Makes 8 to 10 servings. PER EACH OF 10 SERVINGS: about 354 cal, 30 g pro, 18 g total fat (7 g sat. fat), 19 g carb, 4 g fibre, 83 mg chol, 420 mg sodium. % RDI: 8% calcium, 29% iron, 34% vit A, 38% vit C, 21% folate.

Beef Perogies

This filling is the perfect way to use up leftover pot roast or brisket. Boiled and served in soup, these dumplings make a rustic, satisfying meal.

1 tbsp **vegetable oil**

2 **onions,** chopped

8 oz (225 g) **cooked beef pot roast** or brisket, chopped

1 **egg**

½ tsp each **salt** and **pepper**

Savoury Perogy Dough (below)

In skillet, heat oil over medium heat; cook onions, stirring often, until golden, about 10 minutes.

In food processor, pulse together beef, egg, salt and pepper until coarse. Add onions; pulse just until combined.

Working with 1 portion of perogy dough at a time and keeping remainder covered, roll out on lightly floured surface to scant ¼-inch (5 mm) thickness.

Using 3-inch (8 cm) round cutter, cut into rounds. Place 1 tsp filling on each round. Lightly moisten edge of half of round with water; fold over filling and pinch edges together to seal. Place on flour-dusted cloth; cover with tea towel. Repeat with remaining dough and filling, rerolling scraps, to make 36 perogies. (Make-ahead: Freeze in single layer on baking sheet until firm. Transfer to freezer bag; seal and freeze for up to 1 month. Cook from frozen, adding 3 minutes to cooking time.)

In large pot of boiling salted water, cook perogies, in batches and stirring gently, until floating and tender, about 5 minutes. With slotted spoon, transfer to colander to drain.

make your own!

Savoury Perogy Dough

In bowl, whisk 3 cups all-purpose flour with 1 tsp salt. Whisk together 1 egg, ¾ cup water and 2 tbsp vegetable oil; stir into flour mixture, adding up to 2 tbsp more water if needed to make soft but not sticky dough. On lightly floured surface, knead dough until smooth, 10 times. Halve dough; cover with plastic wrap or damp towel. Let rest for 20 minutes.
Makes enough for about 36 perogies.

Makes about 36 pieces. PER PIECE: about 73 cal, 3 g pro, 3 g total fat (1 g sat. fat), 9 g carb, trace fibre, 11 mg chol, 121 mg sodium, 40 mg potassium. % RDI: 5% iron, 11% folate.

EASY
WEEKNIGHT
MEAL

Steak Alla Pizzaiola

Inside round steaks simmered in luscious fresh tomato sauce are toothsome and so economical. Serve over your favourite long pasta.

2 **beef inside round steaks** (each about 12 oz/340 g)

¼ cup **all-purpose flour**

½ tsp each **salt** and **pepper**

2 tbsp **olive oil**

3 cloves **garlic,** crushed

¼ tsp **hot pepper flakes**

⅓ cup **dry red wine**

1 can (28 oz/796 mL) **whole tomatoes**

8 **fresh basil leaves**

¼ tsp **dried oregano**

Cut steaks in half. Between plastic wrap, pound each to about ½-inch (1 cm) thickness.

In shallow dish, whisk together flour and half each of the salt and pepper. Dredge steaks in flour mixture, shaking off excess.

In shallow Dutch oven, heat oil over medium-high heat; brown steaks, turning once, about 2 minutes. Transfer to plate.

Add garlic and hot pepper flakes to pan; cook over medium heat, stirring, for 30 seconds. Add wine; simmer, scraping up browned bits, until reduced to about 2 tbsp, about 1 minute.

Add tomatoes, basil, oregano and remaining salt and pepper, breaking up tomatoes with spoon. Bring to boil; reduce heat and simmer until thickened, about 5 minutes. Return steaks and any accumulated juices to pan; simmer for 4 minutes.

Makes 4 servings. PER SERVING: about 318 cal, 41 g pro, 11 g total fat (3 g sat. fat), 11 g carb, 2 g fibre, 87 mg chol, 435 mg sodium, 1,008 mg potassium. % RDI: 7% calcium, 42% iron, 3% vit A, 47% vit C, 11% folate.

Turkish-Style Stuffed Eggplant

Ground lamb is common in Turkish cuisine and easy to find in many supermarkets. Ground beef is less expensive, and it's just as tasty.

⅓ cup **medium bulgur**

2 **eggplants** (each 1 lb/450 g)

2 tbsp **lemon juice**

1½ tsp **salt**

2 tbsp **olive oil**

1 lb (450 g) **ground lamb** or ground beef

4 cloves **garlic,** minced

2 tbsp **tomato paste**

2 cups diced **Spanish onion** (about half)

1 tsp **ground cumin**

½ tsp **cinnamon**

¼ tsp **cayenne pepper**

¼ cup chopped **fresh parsley**

1 tsp **dried mint**

2 small **tomatoes,** sliced

how-to

Keep It Steady

Slice a small piece off the bottom of each eggplant half to make it sit flat in the baking dish.

In saucepan, bring ¾ cup water to boil; stir in bulgur. Reduce heat to low; cover and cook until no liquid remains, about 10 minutes. Fluff with fork; set aside.

Meanwhile, pressing lightly, roll eggplants over work surface to loosen flesh; cut in half lengthwise. With spoon, scoop out flesh, leaving ½-inch (1 cm) thick shells. Sprinkle shells with 1 tbsp of the lemon juice and ½ tsp of the salt; set aside. Chop flesh.

In skillet, heat 1 tbsp of the oil over medium-high heat; sauté lamb, garlic and ¼ tsp of the remaining salt until lamb is no longer pink. Drain off fat. Add tomato paste; cook until no liquid remains, about 3 minutes. Stir in bulgur, breaking up with spoon; transfer to large bowl.

Heat remaining oil over medium-high heat; sauté chopped eggplant, remaining salt, onion, cumin, cinnamon and cayenne until vegetables are softened and golden, about 5 minutes. Add to lamb mixture. Stir in parsley, mint and remaining lemon juice.

Fill eggplant shells with lamb mixture; place in casserole dish just large enough to hold shells snugly. Lay tomato slices over top. Cover with lightly greased foil. Bake in 400°F (200°C) oven for 1 hour.

Makes 4 to 6 servings. PER EACH OF 6 SERVINGS: about 355 cal, 16 g pro, 22 g total fat (8 g sat. fat), 28 g carb, 6 g fibre, 53 mg chol, 633 mg sodium, 616 mg potassium. % RDI: 5% calcium, 19% iron, 6% vit A, 18% vit C, 21% folate.

Argentinian-Style Grilled Steak & Carrots

Argentinian chimichurri, a flavourful herb mixture, is also nice with grilled chicken or fish. Cover and refrigerate any leftover sauce for up to three days.

4 large **carrots,** cut lengthwise in ¼-inch (5 mm) thick slices

1 tbsp **olive oil**

¼ tsp each **salt** and **pepper**

½ tsp **ground cumin**

1 lb (450 g) **beef marinating flank steak** or beef grilling steak

CHIMICHURRI SAUCE:

¾ cup packed **fresh parsley leaves**

2 **green onions,** chopped

1 small clove **garlic**

2 tbsp **red wine vinegar**

Pinch each **salt** and **pepper**

Pinch **hot pepper flakes**

3 tbsp **extra-virgin olive oil**

In large shallow dish, toss together carrots, 2 tsp of the oil and half each of the salt and pepper; set aside.

Combine cumin and remaining oil, salt and pepper; brush over both sides of steak. Place steak and carrots on greased grill over medium-high heat; close lid and grill, turning once, until steak is medium-rare, about 12 minutes, and carrots are tender, about 16 minutes.

Transfer steak to cutting board; tent with foil. Let stand for 5 minutes before thinly slicing across the grain.

CHIMICHURRI SAUCE: Meanwhile, in food processor, pulse together parsley, green onions, garlic, vinegar, salt, pepper and hot pepper flakes. With motor running, slowly drizzle in oil and 2 tbsp water. Serve with steak and carrots.

Makes 4 servings. PER SERVING: about 323 cal, 25 g pro, 20 g total fat (5 g sat. fat), 9 g carb, 3 g fibre, 48 mg chol, 248 mg sodium, 534 mg potassium. % RDI: 5% calcium, 25% iron, 170% vit A, 33% vit C, 18% folate.

Tomato Chili Flank Steak With Grilled Cauliflower

Keep these common marinade ingredients on hand so you can whip up this low-cost gourmet dinner at a moment's notice.

¼ cup **tomato juice**

2 tbsp packed **brown sugar**

2 tbsp **soy sauce**

1 tbsp **olive oil**

1½ tsp **chili powder**

1 clove **garlic,** minced

Pinch **ground cumin**

1 lb (450 g) **beef marinating flank steak**

Pinch **salt**

GRILLED CAULIFLOWER:

1 small **cauliflower** (about 12 oz/340 g), trimmed

2 tbsp **olive oil**

1 tbsp **lemon juice**

1 tsp **garam masala** or curry powder

Pinch each **salt** and **pepper**

In large shallow dish, whisk together tomato juice, brown sugar, soy sauce, oil, chili powder, garlic and cumin. Add steak, turning to coat. Let stand at room temperature for 10 minutes. *(Make-ahead: Cover and refrigerate for up to 24 hours.)*

GRILLED CAULIFLOWER: Cut cauliflower into bite-size florets; thread onto metal skewers. Whisk together oil, lemon juice, garam masala, salt and pepper; brush over cauliflower. Place on greased grill over medium-high heat; close lid and grill, turning occasionally, until tender-crisp and grill-marked, about 16 minutes.

Meanwhile, remove steak from marinade; scrape marinade into small saucepan. Sprinkle steak with salt. Add to grill; close lid and grill, turning once, until medium-rare, about 8 minutes. Transfer to cutting board; let stand for 5 minutes. Slice thinly across grain.

Meanwhile, bring marinade to boil over medium-high heat; cook, stirring frequently, until reduced to ¼ cup, 3 to 4 minutes. Serve drizzled over steak with cauliflower on the side.

Makes 4 servings. PER SERVING: about 311 cal, 26 g pro, 17 g total fat (4 g sat. fat), 13 g carb, 3 g fibre, 48 mg chol, 573 mg sodium, 459 mg potassium. % RDI: 3% calcium, 21% iron, 4% vit A, 75% vit C, 23% folate.

Five-Spice Chicken
With Ginger Rice,
page 86

chapter two

White Meat

Slow Cooker Barbecue Pork Stew

To make sure the sweet potatoes don't fall apart, push them (and the pork) gently to one side of the cooker, then whisk the flour mixture into the liquid.

3 lb (1.35 kg) **boneless pork shoulder blade roast,** cubed

2 **onions,** chopped

6 cloves **garlic,** minced

2 **bay leaves**

2 tsp **chili powder**

1 tsp each **ground cumin** and **ground coriander**

1 tsp **dried oregano**

½ tsp each **dry mustard, salt** and **pepper**

2 lb (900 g) **sweet potatoes,** peeled, halved and cut in 1½-inch (4 cm) thick slices

1 cup **bottled strained tomatoes** (passata)

1 cup **sodium-reduced chicken broth**

3 tbsp **cooking molasses**

3 tbsp **cider vinegar**

3 tbsp **all-purpose flour**

4 cups packed chopped stemmed **kale**

In slow cooker, combine pork, onions, garlic, bay leaves, chili powder, cumin, coriander, oregano, mustard, salt and pepper; top with sweet potatoes.

Whisk together tomatoes, broth, molasses and vinegar; pour over pork mixture. Cover and cook on low until pork is tender, 6 to 8 hours. Discard bay leaves.

Whisk flour with 1 cup of the cooking liquid until smooth; whisk into slow cooker. Add kale; cook, covered, on high until thickened and kale is wilted, about 30 minutes.

Makes 6 to 8 servings. PER EACH OF 8 SERVINGS: about 572 cal, 33 g pro, 33 g total fat (12 g sat. fat), 35 g carb, 4 g fibre, 119 mg chol, 386 mg sodium, 1,106 mg potassium. % RDI: 11% calcium, 33% iron, 206% vit A, 83% vit C, 16% folate.

BIG BATCH

Turkey Black Bean Chili

Ground turkey or chicken makes a lighter-tasting chili that's a refreshing change from typical beef-based ones. It's wonderful with crusty buns or corn bread.

2 tbsp **vegetable oil**

1 lb (450 g) **ground turkey**
   or chicken

1 **onion,** chopped

2 cloves **garlic,** minced

2 tsp **dried oregano**

½ tsp **salt**

¼ tsp **pepper**

2 tbsp **tomato paste**

1 can (28 oz/796 mL) **diced
   tomatoes**

1 can (19 oz/540 mL) **black beans,**
   drained and rinsed

1 small **zucchini,** cubed

½ cup **frozen corn kernels**

3 tbsp **chili powder**

¼ cup minced **fresh cilantro**
   or parsley

Sour cream and sliced **jalapeño
   peppers** (optional)

In large saucepan, heat 1 tbsp of the oil over medium-high heat; cook turkey, breaking up with spoon, until no longer pink, about 8 minutes. Using slotted spoon, transfer turkey to bowl.

Drain fat from pan; heat remaining oil over medium heat. Cook onion, garlic, oregano, salt and pepper until softened, about 3 minutes. Stir in tomato paste; cook for 1 minute.

Return turkey to pan. Add tomatoes, black beans, zucchini, corn and chili powder; bring to boil. Reduce heat and simmer for 30 minutes. Stir in cilantro. Serve garnished with sour cream and jalapeño peppers (if using).

Makes 4 to 6 servings. PER EACH OF 6 SERVINGS: about 281 cal, 20 g pro, 12 g total fat (3 g sat. fat), 26 g carb, 9 g fibre, 60 mg chol, 717 mg sodium. % RDI: 9% calcium, 33% iron, 16% vit A, 42% vit C, 30% folate.

Sausage & Spinach Soup With Rosemary Croutons

Day-old bread makes the best croutons; they're a terrific, old-fashioned money saver. Serve this quick version of Italian wedding soup with a green salad.

2 tbsp **olive oil**

12 oz (340 g) **mild Italian sausages,** casings removed

2 cloves **garlic,** minced

Half **onion,** finely diced

1 tsp **dried rosemary**

¼ tsp **pepper**

3 cups **sodium-reduced chicken broth**

⅔ cup **tubetti pasta**

6 cups **baby spinach**

2 cups cubed **day-old Italian bread** or day-old baguette

2 tbsp grated **Parmesan cheese**

In large saucepan, heat 1 tsp of the oil over medium-high heat; cook sausage meat, breaking up with spoon, until browned, 5 to 6 minutes. With slotted spoon, remove sausage and set aside.

Drain fat from pan; cook garlic, onion and half each of the rosemary and pepper, stirring occasionally, until onion is softened, about 2 minutes.

Add broth and 3 cups water. Return sausage to pan; cover and bring to boil. Add pasta; reduce heat to medium and cook until pasta is al dente, about 8 minutes. Turn off heat. Add baby spinach; stir just until wilted.

Meanwhile, toss bread with remaining oil, rosemary and pepper; spread on baking sheet. Bake in 375°F (190°C) oven until golden, 10 minutes. Serve soup sprinkled with croutons and Parmesan cheese.

change it up!

Spicy Sausage & Spinach Soup With Rosemary Croutons

Dial up the heat by substituting hot Italian sausages for the mild and adding ¼ tsp hot pepper flakes to the soup along with the rosemary and pepper.

Makes 4 to 6 servings. PER EACH OF 6 SERVINGS: about 276 cal, 15 g pro, 14 g total fat (4 g sat. fat), 22 g carb, 2 g fibre, 26 mg chol, 768 mg sodium, 246 mg potassium. % RDI: 9% calcium, 19% iron, 31% vit A, 7% vit C, 41% folate.

SMART
CHOICE

Slow Cooker Souper Chicken Noodle Soup

Lower in sodium than canned soups, this classic is satisfying to body and soul. Kale contains vitamins A and C, folic acid, calcium and iron.

2 **onions,** chopped

2 ribs **celery,** chopped

2 **carrots,** chopped

2 **sweet potatoes** (about 1¼ lb/ 565 g), peeled and chopped

2 slices **fresh ginger**

1 tsp **salt**

½ tsp **pepper**

6 **bone-in chicken thighs** (about 2 lb/900 g)

3½ cups **Easy No-Salt-Added Chicken Stock** (below) or no-salt-added chicken broth

3 cups sliced stemmed **kale**

2 cups **curly egg noodles**

½ cup **frozen peas**

In slow cooker, combine onions, celery, carrots, sweet potatoes, ginger, salt and pepper. Arrange chicken over vegetables. Pour in stock and 3 cups water. Cover and cook on low for 6 to 8 hours.

Transfer chicken to bowl. Stir kale, noodles and peas into soup. Cover and cook on high until noodles are tender, about 30 minutes.

Meanwhile, remove and discard chicken skin, bones and fat. Shred or chop meat; return to soup.

make your own!

Easy No-Salt-Added Chicken Stock

In slow cooker, combine 2 lb (900 g) chicken bones (carcasses, wings and necks); 2 onions, coarsely chopped; 3 ribs celery, coarsely chopped; 3 carrots, coarsely chopped; 10 sprigs parsley or leftover stems; 2 bay leaves; and ½ tsp black peppercorns. Pour in 12 cups cold water. Cover and cook on low for 12 to 24 hours. Strain through cheesecloth–lined sieve into large bowl, pressing vegetables to extract liquid. Let cool for 30 minutes. Refrigerate, uncovered, until fat hardens on surface, about 8 hours. Save fat for another use or discard. *(Make-ahead: Refrigerate in airtight containers for up to 3 days or freeze for up to 2 months.)* **Makes 12 cups.**

Makes 8 servings. PER SERVING: about 285 cal, 17 g pro, 12 g total fat (4 g sat. fat), 26 g carb, 4 g fibre, 61 mg chol, 391 mg sodium, 523 mg potassium. % RDI: 6% calcium, 15% iron, 156% vit A, 45% vit C, 13% folate.

Chicken Fricot

Fricot, an Acadian stew made with meat or fish and topped with fluffy "doughboy" dumplings, is the ultimate comfort food. It's a great way to use up a whole chicken, but a mix of thighs and drumsticks is even cheaper and just as delicious.

1 **whole chicken** (about 3 lb/ 1.35 kg) or 3 lb (1.35 kg) chicken thighs and drumsticks

4 oz (115 g) **salt pork,** diced

3 **carrots,** chopped

3 ribs **celery,** chopped

1 large **onion,** chopped

2 lb (900 g) **yellow-fleshed potatoes,** peeled and chopped

2 tsp **dried savory**

¾ tsp **salt**

½ tsp **pepper**

2 **ice cubes**

DUMPLINGS:

1½ cups **all-purpose flour**

1 tbsp **baking powder**

1 tbsp chopped **fresh parsley**

½ tsp **salt**

2 **egg yolks**

Discarding back, cut chicken into 6 pieces. In Dutch oven, sauté salt pork over medium-high heat until golden, 4 minutes. With slotted spoon, transfer pork to plate. Add chicken to pan; brown all over, about 8 minutes. Add to plate with pork; set aside.

Drain all but 2 tbsp fat from pan; cook carrots, celery and onion over medium heat, stirring often, until onion is softened, about 3 minutes.

Stir in potatoes, savory, salt and pepper; cook, stirring, for 2 minutes. Return chicken and pork to pan; stir in 6 cups water. Bring to boil, skimming off foam. Reduce heat, cover and simmer for 45 minutes.

Place ice cubes in glass measure. Pour in enough of the cooking liquid to make ⅔ cup; let cool.

Meanwhile, with slotted spoon, transfer chicken to plate; let cool enough to handle. Pull meat from bones; discard bones and skin. Shred or coarsely chop chicken. Skim any fat from cooking liquid; return chicken to pan and bring to simmer.

DUMPLINGS: In bowl, whisk flour, baking powder, parsley and salt. Stir egg yolks into reserved cooking liquid; drizzle over flour mixture. With fork, toss to make sticky, stretchy dough.

Drop batter, evenly spaced in 8 mounds, onto stew; cover and simmer over medium heat until puffed and knife inserted into centre of dumplings comes out clean, 8 to 10 minutes.

Makes 8 servings. PER SERVING: about 395 cal, 20 g pro, 16 g total fat, 4 g sat. fat, 42 g carb, 3 g fibre, 110 mg chol, 757 mg sodium, 640 mg potassium. % RDI: 9% calcium, 19% iron, 53% vit A, 15% vit C, 35% folate.

Slow Cooker Smoked Turkey & Sweet Potato Soup

Smoked turkey is full of flavour and stays tender and moist when prepared in a slow cooker. Simmering it on the bone creates a delicious, rich-tasting broth.

1 **smoked turkey leg** or smoked turkey thigh (about 18 oz/510 g)

3 **sweet potatoes** (2 lb/900 g), peeled and chopped

2 **onions,** chopped

1 rib **celery,** chopped

2 cloves **garlic,** minced

1½ tsp **Cajun seasoning**

1 tbsp **cider vinegar**

Trim fat from turkey. In slow cooker, combine turkey, sweet potatoes, onions, celery, garlic and Cajun seasoning; pour in 6 cups water.

Cover and cook on low for 6 to 8 hours. Transfer turkey to cutting board; let cool slightly.

Transfer 3 cups of the soup to blender; purée until smooth. Return to slow cooker; stir in vinegar.

Remove and discard skin, bones and fat from turkey. Shred or chop meat and return to soup.

Makes 10 servings. PER SERVING: about 134 cal, 11 g pro, 3 g total fat (1 g sat. fat), 17 g carb, 3 g fibre, 27 mg chol, 402 mg sodium, 330 mg potassium. % RDI: 4% calcium, 11% iron, 127% vit A, 18% vit C, 5% folate.

Slow Cooker Butter Chicken

You can leave this recipe simmering in a slow cooker for eight hours before adding the chicken. It yields a large quantity of sauce that freezes well if you're feeding a smaller group. Serve over hot steamed basmati rice.

2 **onions,** diced

3 cloves **garlic,** minced

3 tbsp **butter**

2 tbsp grated **fresh ginger**

2 tbsp packed **brown sugar**

2 tsp **chili powder**

¾ tsp each **ground coriander** and **turmeric**

½ tsp each **cinnamon** and **ground cumin**

½ tsp each **salt** and **pepper**

1 can (28 oz/796 mL) **diced tomatoes**

1 cup **sodium-reduced chicken broth**

¼ cup **almond butter** or cashew butter

3 lb (1.35 kg) **boneless skinless chicken thighs,** quartered

1 cup **sour cream**

2 tbsp chopped **fresh cilantro**

In slow cooker, combine onions, garlic, butter, ginger, brown sugar, chili powder, coriander, turmeric, cinnamon, cumin, salt, pepper and tomatoes. Whisk broth with almond butter; pour into slow cooker.

Cover and cook on low for 5 hours or for up to 8 hours.

With immersion blender, purée sauce until smooth. Add chicken; cook, covered, on high until juices run clear when chicken is pierced, 30 to 40 minutes.

Stir in sour cream. Serve sprinkled with cilantro.

Makes 8 servings. PER SERVING: about 398 cal, 36 g pro, 22 g total fat (8 g sat. fat), 14 g carb, 2 g fibre, 164 mg chol, 580 mg sodium, 766 mg potassium. % RDI: 11% calcium, 26% iron, 13% vit A, 32% vit C, 13% folate.

BETTER
THAN
TAKEOUT!

Braised Pork Shoulder & White Beans

Braising a humble pork shoulder roast makes it meltingly tender. The acidity of the garlic vinegar tempers the richness of the pork – add it to taste at the table.

2 cups **dried navy beans** or
    cannellini beans (1 lb/450 g)

4 lb (1.8 kg) **bone-in pork shoulder
picnic roast** (fat cap on) or
boneless pork butt roast

1 tsp each **salt** and **pepper** (approx)

1 tbsp **extra-virgin olive oil**

3 ribs **celery,** diced

2 **carrots,** diced

1 **onion,** diced

5 cloves **garlic,** minced

1 tsp **dried thyme**

½ tsp **dried oregano**

1 **bay leaf**

GARLIC VINEGAR:

2 cloves **garlic,** minced

¼ cup **white wine vinegar**

Pinch **salt**

Rinse and soak beans overnight in 3 times their volume of water. (Or bring to boil and boil gently for 2 minutes. Remove from heat, cover and let stand for 1 hour.) Drain.

In saucepan, cover beans with 3 times their volume of fresh water; bring to boil. Reduce heat, cover and simmer until tender, about 40 minutes. Reserving 2½ cups of the cooking liquid, drain.

Sprinkle pork all over with salt and pepper. In Dutch oven, heat oil over high heat; brown pork all over. Transfer to plate.

Drain all but 1 tbsp fat from pan; cook celery, carrots and onion over medium heat until softened and light golden, about 8 minutes. Stir in garlic, thyme, oregano and bay leaf; cook for 2 minutes.

Add beans to pan. Return pork and any accumulated juices to pan. Add reserved bean cooking liquid; bring to boil.

Cover and roast in 350°F (180°C) oven for 2½ hours. Uncover; roast until tender, about 30 minutes. Transfer pork to cutting board; slice. Discard bay leaf.

GARLIC VINEGAR: Meanwhile, whisk together garlic, vinegar and salt. Serve with pork and white beans.

Makes 8 servings. PER SERVING: about 564 cal, 43 g pro, 28 g total fat (9 g sat. fat), 35 g carb, 10 g fibre, 121 mg chol, 449 mg sodium, 1,333 mg potassium. % RDI: 12% calcium, 49% iron, 33% vit A, 7% vit C, 50% folate.

Slow Cooker Smoked Turkey & Noodle Soup

Smoked turkey legs are quite large, so one goes a long way in this homey soup. Use whatever short pasta you prefer – tubetti is another nice alternative.

1 **smoked turkey leg** (about 1 lb/450 g)

1½ cups each chopped **carrots** and **celery**

1 cup sliced **mushrooms**

1 **onion,** diced

2 sprigs **fresh parsley**

1 **bay leaf**

½ tsp each **dried thyme** and **pepper**

3 cups **sodium-reduced chicken broth**

1 **sweet red pepper,** diced

½ cup **frozen peas**

2 cups **small pasta,** such as ditali, mini bow ties or macaroni

Remove skin and meat from turkey leg. Reserve bone; discard skin. Cut meat into bite-size pieces; set aside.

In slow cooker, combine carrots, celery, mushrooms, onion, parsley, bay leaf, thyme and pepper. Add turkey bone, broth and 3 cups water. Cover and cook on low until vegetables are tender, about 6 hours.

Add red pepper, peas and turkey meat. Cover and cook on high until vegetables are tender-crisp, about 15 minutes.

Meanwhile, in saucepan of boiling salted water, cook pasta until al dente; drain. Discard bay leaf and parsley from soup. Stir in pasta.

don't waste it!

Use Up a Larger Leg

If a large turkey leg is all you can find, cut up all the meat and use 2 cups for this soup. Add the rest to pastas, salads or sandwiches.

Makes 8 to 10 servings. PER EACH OF 10 SERVINGS: about 108 cal, 10 g pro, 2 g total fat (1 g sat. fat), 13 g carb, 2 g fibre, 23 mg chol, 266 mg sodium. % RDI: 3% calcium, 10% iron, 36% vit A, 37% vit C, 17% folate.

RECIPE
BOX
ESSENTIAL

Hunter's Chicken With Creamy Polenta

Savoury, saucy and perfect for a cold night, this stew offers plenty of protein from the chicken and beans. Polenta is the ultimate inexpensive side dish.

1 tbsp **olive oil**

8 **boneless skinless chicken thighs** (about 1½ lb/675 g), cut in 1-inch (2.5 cm) chunks

1 **onion,** chopped

8 oz (225 g) **button mushrooms,** sliced

3 cloves **garlic,** minced

1 cup **sodium-reduced chicken broth**

1 cup **bottled strained tomatoes** (passata)

1 can (19 oz/540 mL) **white kidney beans,** drained and rinsed

1 tbsp **tomato paste**

2 tsp **dried Italian herb seasoning**

Pinch **salt**

¼ cup chopped **fresh parsley**

CREAMY POLENTA:

1⅔ cups **cornmeal**

¼ tsp each **salt** and **pepper**

¼ cup **butter,** cubed

In large nonstick skillet, heat 2 tsp of the oil over medium-high heat; brown chicken, about 8 minutes. Transfer to plate.

In same skillet, heat remaining oil over medium heat; cook onion, stirring occasionally, until softened, about 5 minutes. Add mushrooms and garlic; cook, stirring occasionally, for 3 minutes.

Stir in chicken broth, tomatoes, beans, tomato paste, Italian herb seasoning, salt, and chicken and any accumulated juices; bring to boil. Reduce heat and simmer until thickened, about 15 minutes Stir in parsley.

CREAMY POLENTA: Meanwhile, in large saucepan, bring 6 cups water to boil. Whisk in cornmeal, salt and pepper; simmer over medium-low heat, stirring often, until thick and stiff to stir, about 10 minutes. Stir in butter.

Makes 4 servings. PER SERVING: about 708 cal, 46 g pro, 26 g total fat (10 g sat. fat), 72 g carb, 13 g fibre, 172 mg chol, 961 mg sodium, 1,104 mg potassium. % RDI: 9% calcium, 44% iron, 18% vit A, 23% vit C, 65% folate.

Chicken Paprikash

This Hungarian dish is traditionally simmered for quite a while. Using chunks of boneless chicken thighs cuts down on time while still adding lots of flavour.

2 tbsp **olive oil**

1 lb (450 g) **boneless skinless chicken thighs,** quartered

1 **onion,** thinly sliced

3 cloves **garlic,** minced

2½ cups sliced trimmed **cremini mushrooms**

2 tbsp **sweet paprika**

3 tbsp **all-purpose flour**

2 tbsp **tomato paste**

2 cups **sodium-reduced chicken broth**

1 tsp **lemon juice**

½ tsp **salt**

Pinch **pepper**

1 pkg (375 g) **broad egg noodles**

½ cup **light sour cream**

2 tbsp chopped **fresh parsley**

In large nonstick skillet, heat 1 tbsp of the oil over medium-high heat; brown chicken, 4 to 5 minutes. With slotted spoon, transfer to plate.

Drain fat from pan; heat remaining oil over medium heat. Cook onion, garlic, mushrooms and paprika, stirring often, until onion is softened, 1 to 2 minutes.

Add flour and tomato paste; cook, stirring, for 1 minute. Gradually stir in broth and bring to boil; reduce heat and simmer until thickened, about 1 minute. Return chicken and accumulated juices to pan; add lemon juice, salt and pepper.

Meanwhile, in saucepan of boiling salted water, cook noodles according to package directions. Drain noodles; serve topped with chicken mixture. Garnish with sour cream and parsley.

Makes 4 servings. PER SERVING: about 676 cal, 40 g pro, 20 g total fat (4 g sat. fat), 84 g carb, 7 g fibre, 176 mg chol, 1,159 mg sodium, 873 mg potassium. % RDI: 13% calcium, 52% iron, 23% vit A, 17% vit C, 135% folate.

Creamy Turkey Chowder

If you have turkey broth in the freezer (post-holiday, usually), use it to add exceptional flavour to this hearty, low-maintenance soup. It's a wonderful way to enjoy leftovers.

2 tbsp **butter**

2 **carrots,** diced

2 ribs **celery,** diced

1 **onion,** diced

8 oz (225 g) **yellow-fleshed potato** (1 large), peeled and diced

½ tsp each **dried thyme** and **salt**

¼ tsp each crumbled **dried sage** and **pepper**

¼ cup **all-purpose flour**

2 cups **sodium-reduced chicken broth**

2 cups diced **cooked turkey**

1½ cups **milk**

In large Dutch oven, heat butter over medium heat; cook carrots, celery, onion, potato, thyme, salt, sage and pepper, stirring occasionally, until onion is softened, about 6 minutes.

Stir in flour; cook, stirring, for 2 minutes. Whisk in broth and 2 cups water; bring to boil. Reduce heat, cover and simmer until potatoes are tender, about 15 minutes.

Stir in turkey and milk and bring just to simmer (do not boil); simmer gently until heated through, about 5 minutes.

Makes 4 servings. PER SERVING: about 318 cal, 28 g pro, 11 g total fat (6 g sat. fat), 26 g carb, 3 g fibre, 76 mg chol, 751 mg sodium, 686 mg potassium. % RDI: 15% calcium, 16% iron, 74% vit A, 12% vit C, 19% folate.

Sri Lankan Devil's Chicken

Look for fresh curry leaves in Asian markets (freeze any leftovers in a resealable bag for up to three months). If you can't find them, this spicy dish is still extremely delicious without them. Serve with steamed basmati rice.

8 **chicken drumsticks**

¾ tsp **salt**

½ tsp **turmeric**

¼ cup **malt vinegar** or cider vinegar

4 tsp **tomato paste**

2 tsp **granulated sugar**

1 tsp **cayenne pepper**

1 large clove **garlic,** minced

½ tsp **hot paprika**

5 **dried red hot peppers**

3 tbsp **vegetable oil**

2 cups chopped **onion**

3 **green onions,** cut in large chunks

1 **red finger hot pepper,**
     thinly sliced

1 **green finger hot pepper,**
     thinly sliced

10 **fresh curry leaves**

1 **cinnamon stick**

2 cups chopped **tomato**

Pat chicken dry. Sprinkle with three-quarters of the salt, and the turmeric; cover and refrigerate for 30 minutes.

Stir together vinegar, tomato paste, sugar, cayenne pepper, garlic, paprika, remaining salt and ¼ cup water. In mortar with pestle, pound dried hot peppers until broken. Set hot peppers and vinegar mixture aside separately.

In wok or large skillet, heat 1 tbsp of the oil over medium heat; brown chicken, in batches if necessary, about 15 minutes. Transfer to plate.

Increase heat to medium-high; add remaining oil to pan. Sauté chopped onion until golden, about 5 minutes. Add pounded hot peppers; stir in green onions, red and green hot peppers, curry leaves and cinnamon; cook until vegetables are softened, about 2 minutes.

Add tomato; return chicken and any accumulated juices to pan. Stir in vinegar mixture; cover and simmer, stirring occasionally, for 15 minutes.

Uncover and cook until thickened, about 5 minutes. Remove cinnamon stick.

buy in bulk

Economy Packs

You'll often find large trays of chicken drumsticks on sale. Buy them when the price is good and freeze them to use later in stews like this, or grill them up at a backyard barbecue.

Makes 4 servings. PER SERVING: about 410 cal, 25 g pro, 27 g total fat (5 g sat. fat), 18 g carb, 3 g fibre, 105 mg chol, 553 mg sodium, 745 mg potassium. % RDI: 5% calcium, 18% iron, 19% vit A, 38% vit C, 17% folate.

FOR SPICE LOVERS

Pork & Grainy Mustard Stew

Rich stews like this develop even more flavour as they sit in the refrigerator, making them perfect to reheat later in the week.

3 lb (1.35 kg) **pork braising cubes** or boneless pork shoulder blade roast, trimmed and cubed

2 tbsp **all-purpose flour**

3 tbsp **vegetable oil**

2 **onions,** chopped

4 **carrots,** chopped

2 ribs **celery,** chopped

2 cloves **garlic,** minced

1 tsp **dried thyme**

¼ tsp each **salt** and **pepper**

2 cups **sodium-reduced chicken broth**

½ cup **white wine** or sodium-reduced chicken broth

1 **bay leaf**

¼ cup **grainy mustard**

¾ cup **frozen peas**

¼ cup minced **fresh parsley**

Toss pork with 1 tbsp of the flour. In Dutch oven, heat half of the oil over medium-high heat; brown pork, in batches and adding more oil as needed. Transfer to plate.

In same pan, heat remaining oil; fry onions, carrots, celery, garlic, thyme, salt and pepper, stirring occasionally, until softened, about 5 minutes.

Add broth, wine, bay leaf and 1½ cups water; return pork and any accumulated juices to pan. Bring to boil; reduce heat, cover and simmer, stirring occasionally, until meat is tender, about 45 minutes. Discard bay leaf.

Whisk together mustard, remaining flour and 2 tbsp water; stir into stew. Simmer until thickened, about 3 minutes. Stir in peas and parsley; cook until heated through, about 3 minutes. *(Make-ahead: Let cool for 30 minutes. Refrigerate, uncovered, in shallow container until cold. Cover and refrigerate for up to 3 days. Or freeze for up to 1 month; thaw in refrigerator.)*

Makes 8 servings. PER SERVING: about 315 cal, 37 g pro, 13 g total fat (3 g sat. fat), 11 g carb, 2 g fibre, 109 mg chol, 480 mg sodium. % RDI: 5% calcium, 23% iron, 69% vit A, 12% vit C, 15% folate.

Pork & Shiitake Lettuce Wraps

Boston lettuce makes the perfect wrap for this pork stir-fry, although leaf lettuce is a good substitute.

1 tbsp **hoisin sauce**

1 tsp **cornstarch**

1 lb (450 g) **lean ground pork**

1 tsp **vegetable oil**

2 tsp grated **fresh ginger**

2 cloves **garlic,** minced

1 **sweet red pepper,** diced

1 cup **shiitake mushroom caps,** thinly sliced

½ cup drained **canned sliced water chestnuts,** chopped

1 rib **celery,** diced

¼ tsp each **salt** and **pepper**

2 **green onions,** thinly sliced

12 leaves **Boston lettuce**

Combine hoisin sauce, cornstarch and ½ cup water; set aside.

In large nonstick skillet, cook pork over medium-high heat, breaking up with spoon, until no longer pink, about 6 minutes. Using slotted spoon, transfer pork to bowl.

Drain fat from pan; add oil. Sauté ginger and garlic until fragrant, about 1 minute. Add red pepper, mushrooms, water chestnuts, celery, salt and pepper; sauté until red pepper and celery are tender-crisp, about 3 minutes.

Return pork to pan, stirring to combine. Stir in hoisin mixture; cook, stirring, until thickened and glossy, about 1 minute. Toss with green onions. Serve in lettuce cups.

Makes 4 servings. PER SERVING: about 248 cal, 23 g pro, 13 g total fat (5 g sat. fat), 10 g carb, 2 g fibre, 66 mg chol, 288 mg sodium, 543 mg potassium. % RDI: 3% calcium, 14% iron, 20% vit A, 87% vit C, 16% folate.

Budget-Friendly White Meat

What Makes It Affordable: With the current emphasis on healthy eating, many people are cooking with lean chicken and turkey breasts exclusively. This means the fattier legs – and their parts, the thighs and drumsticks – are less in demand and therefore cheaper. These dark meats do contain more fat than breasts, but they also offer more luscious flavour, and more iron and vitamin A.

Ground chicken, turkey and pork are another economical choice because they're ground from smaller pieces that aren't useful on their own. Versatile pork chops and fattier pork shoulder roasts are more reasonably priced per pound than tenderloin and offer more flavour than leaner cuts.

Why It's Good for You: Chicken and pork are sources of protein, vitamins B_6 and B_{12}, zinc and niacin. Both contain iron, as well as a variety of other vitamins and minerals in smaller amounts.

Food Safety: Chicken and pork need to be handled carefully to prevent harmful bacteria from making you sick. It's vital to cook these meats – especially the ground versions – to the proper temperature. For pork, that means until an instant-read thermometer inserted into the thickest part reads 160°F (71°C). For poultry legs and ground meat, the temperature needs to be higher, at 165°F (74°C).

Always put cooked meat on a clean plate (not the one the raw meat was on) and chill any leftovers within two hours of cooking. Thaw frozen chicken or pork in the refrigerator, not at room temperature, on a plate to catch the juices. Plan for about a day for small cuts and ground meats to thaw.

Uses: All of these budget-friendly cuts are wonderful grilled. Try ground meats in kabobs, meat loaves and burgers. Chicken legs and thighs lend themselves particularly well to braised and stewed dishes, yielding moist, tender results. Pork chops are terrific on their own or cooked with vegetables to make a one-pot skillet dinner. Pork shoulder makes the best pulled pork, but it's also wonderful cubed and braised in stews, especially with vegetables and legumes.

Pork Burgers

Fresh off the grill, juicy pork burgers topped with gooey Gruyère cheese can stand up to any beef burger. The patties shrink as they cook, so try to make them slightly larger in diameter than the buns.

2 **green onions,** chopped

2 tbsp **Dijon mustard**

2 cloves **garlic,** minced

1 tsp each **dried sage** and **dried rosemary**

½ tsp each **salt** and **pepper**

1 lb (450 g) **lean ground pork**

4 oz (115 g) **Gruyère cheese,** shredded

1 **red onion,** cut in 4 rings

2 tsp **olive oil**

4 **hamburger buns**

In large bowl, combine green onions, mustard, garlic, sage, rosemary and half each of the salt and pepper. Mix in pork; shape into 4 patties.

Place on greased grill over medium-high heat; close lid and grill, turning once, until instant-read thermometer inserted sideways into centre reads 160°F (71°C), about 15 minutes. Top burgers with cheese; cook, covered, until melted, about 1 minute.

Meanwhile, brush onion all over with oil; sprinkle with remaining salt and pepper. Grill, covered and turning once, until softened, about 10 minutes.

Sandwich burgers and onion rings in buns.

Makes 4 servings. PER SERVING: about 506 cal, 36 g pro, 26 g total fat (11 g sat. fat), 32 g carb, 2 g fibre, 97 mg chol, 796 mg sodium, 509 mg potassium. % RDI: 37% calcium, 24% iron, 10% vit A, 10% vit C, 39% folate.

CLASSIC
WITH
A TWIST

Chicken Burgers

Ground chicken is a light-tasting base for these herbed patties. They are quick to make and freeze well, so mix up a bunch when ground chicken is on sale.

1 **egg**

2 tbsp **lemon juice**

1 small **onion,** grated

¼ cup **dry bread crumbs**

2 tsp chopped **fresh thyme**

½ tsp each **salt** and **pepper**

1 lb (450 g) **lean ground chicken**
    or turkey

4 **hamburger buns**

In bowl, beat together egg, 2 tbsp water and lemon juice. Stir in onion, bread crumbs, thyme, salt and pepper; mix in chicken. Shape into four ½-inch (1 cm) thick patties. *(Make-ahead: Layer between waxed paper in airtight container and refrigerate for up to 24 hours or freeze for up to 1 month. Thaw in refrigerator.)*

Place on greased grill over medium-high heat; close lid and grill, turning once, until instant-read thermometer inserted sideways into centre reads 165°F (74°C), about 10 minutes. Sandwich in buns.

Makes 4 servings. PER SERVING: about 401 cal, 29 g pro, 14 g total fat (3 g sat. fat), 37 g carb, 2 g fibre, 126 mg chol, 762 mg sodium. % RDI: 11% calcium, 26% iron, 4% vit A, 5% vit C, 36% folate.

Chili Pulled Pork

This Mexican take on pulled pork is made with mostly pantry staples.
The chocolate in the sauce makes it rich and uniquely complex.

2 tbsp **vegetable oil**

3 lb (1.35 kg) **boneless pork shoulder blade roast**

1½ tsp **salt**

3 **onions,** chopped

4 cloves **garlic,** minced

1½ cups **bottled strained tomatoes** (passata)

⅓ cup **cider vinegar**

¼ cup **chili powder**

¼ cup **fancy molasses**

2 tbsp packed **dark brown sugar**

1 tsp **dried oregano**

1 tsp each **ground cumin** and **ground coriander**

¼ tsp **pepper**

1 oz (30 g) **unsweetened chocolate,** chopped

In Dutch oven, heat oil over medium-high heat. Sprinkle pork with 1 tsp of the salt; brown pork all over. Transfer to plate.

Drain all but 1 tbsp fat from pan; cook onions and garlic, stirring occasionally, until softened, about 5 minutes.

Add tomatoes, 1 cup water, vinegar, chili powder, molasses, brown sugar, oregano, cumin, coriander, pepper and remaining salt; bring to boil, scraping up browned bits. Stir in chocolate until melted.

Return pork and any accumulated juices to pan; bring to boil. Cover and braise in 300°F (150°C) oven, turning once, until tender, about 3 hours.

Transfer pork to large bowl and tent with foil; let stand for 15 minutes. With forks, shred or "pull" pork, discarding skin and fat.

Skim fat from sauce. Return pork to sauce. Heat until bubbly.

change it up!

Chili Braised Brisket

Replace pork with 4 lb (1.8 kg) beef brisket. Omit browning. Place brisket in roasting pan; pour sauce over top, turning to coat. Cover and braise in 325°F (160°C) oven until fork-tender, about 3½ hours. Remove from pan and tent with foil; let stand for 10 minutes before slicing across the grain. Serve with sauce. **Makes 8 to 10 servings.**

Makes 6 servings. PER SERVING: about 628 cal, 41 g pro, 39 g total fat (32 g sat. fat), 30 g carb, 4 g fibre, 153 mg chol, 1,018 mg sodium, 1,189 mg potassium. % RDI: 13% calcium, 48% iron, 18% vit A, 12% vit C, 11% folate.

Pork Kofta Pitas With Tomato Salsa

These filling dinner sandwiches feature a fresh tomato salsa – perfect for using up the bounty from the garden during tomato season.

1 lb (450 g) **lean ground pork**

2 **green onions,** minced

2 cloves **garlic,** minced

2 tbsp minced **fresh dill**

1½ tsp each **sweet paprika** and **ground coriander**

¾ tsp each **salt** and **ground cumin**

1 **egg,** beaten

4 **pitas** (with pockets), cut in half

1 cup sliced **English cucumber**

Half small **red onion,** thinly sliced

TOMATO SALSA:

1 cup chopped seeded **tomatoes** (about 3)

1 **green onion,** thinly sliced

1 tbsp minced **fresh dill**

1 tbsp each **lemon juice** and **extra-virgin olive oil**

Pinch each **salt** and **granulated sugar**

TOMATO SALSA: Combine tomatoes, green onion, dill, lemon juice, oil, salt and sugar; let stand for 10 minutes.

Meanwhile, mix together pork, green onions, garlic, dill, 1 tbsp water, paprika, coriander, salt, cumin and egg. Divide into 8 portions; form each into egg shape. Thread onto metal or soaked wooden skewers.

Place on greased grill over medium heat; close lid and grill, turning once, until instant-read thermometer inserted into several reads 160°F (71°C), about 10 minutes. Remove from skewers. Insert 1 kofta into each pita half; add cucumber, onion and tomato salsa.

Makes 4 servings. PER SERVING: about 433 cal, 29 g pro, 17 g total fat (5 g sat. fat), 40 g carb, 3 g fibre, 119 mg chol, 833 mg sodium, 620 mg potassium. % RDI: 10% calcium, 27% iron, 11% vit A, 20% vit C, 44% folate.

Five-Spice Chicken With Ginger Rice

With only seven ingredients in the chicken and four in the rice, this dinner couldn't be simpler to prepare. Serve with a tossed salad or a steamed green vegetable.

2 tbsp **lemon juice**

2 tbsp **vegetable oil**

2 tsp **liquid honey**

1 tsp **five-spice powder**

¼ tsp each **salt** and **pepper**

8 **chicken drumsticks** and/or **thighs**

GINGER RICE:

1 cup **jasmine rice** or other long-grain rice

6 slices **fresh ginger**

¼ tsp **salt**

1 **green onion** (green part only), minced

In large bowl, whisk together lemon juice, 1 tbsp of the oil, honey, five-spice powder, salt and pepper. Remove skin from chicken, if desired. Add chicken to marinade, turning to coat; let stand for 5 minutes. Discard any remaining marinade.

In ovenproof skillet, heat remaining oil over medium-high heat; brown chicken, in batches. Drain fat from pan.

Return all chicken to skillet. Roast in 425°F (220°C) oven until juices run clear when chicken is pierced, about 30 minutes.

GINGER RICE: Meanwhile, in saucepan, bring 1½ cups water, rice, ginger and salt to boil. Reduce heat to low; cover and simmer until rice is tender and no liquid remains, about 20 minutes. Stir in green onion. Serve with chicken.

Makes 4 servings. PER SERVING (WITHOUT SKIN): about 447 cal, 30 g pro, 17 g total fat (3 g sat. fat), 42 g carb, 1 g fibre, 94 mg chol, 373 mg sodium. % RDI: 3% calcium, 11% iron, 3% vit A, 4% vit C, 6% folate.

Yogurt-Spiced Chicken With Grilled Tomato Kabobs

To save time, you can make the chicken a day ahead and marinate it overnight. Sprinkle with cilantro (if desired) and serve with grilled naan or Greek-style pitas.

¼ cup **2% plain yogurt**

2 tbsp **lemon juice**

1 tbsp grated **fresh ginger**

1 tbsp **tomato paste**

2 cloves **garlic,** grated

2 tsp **garam masala**

½ tsp **salt**

1 lb (450 g) **boneless skinless chicken thighs**

1 tbsp **olive oil**

2 cups **cherry tomatoes**

Half **red onion,** cut in ¾-inch (2 cm) chunks

In shallow dish, combine yogurt, 1 tbsp of the lemon juice, ginger, tomato paste, garlic, 1½ tsp of the garam masala and ¼ tsp of the salt. Add chicken, tossing to coat; let stand for 15 minutes. *(Make-ahead: Cover and refrigerate for up to 24 hours.)*

Meanwhile, combine oil and remaining lemon juice, garam masala and salt; set aside. Alternately thread tomatoes and onion onto metal skewers.

Place chicken on greased grill over medium-high heat; close lid and grill, turning halfway through, until juices run clear when chicken is pierced, about 4 minutes.

Meanwhile, add skewers; grill, turning 4 times and brushing with oil mixture, until onion is slightly softened and tomatoes are slightly charred, about 4 minutes. Serve with chicken.

time-saver

Skip the Soaking Step

Using metal skewers means you don't have to soak them in advance, the way you would with wooden skewers.

Makes 4 servings. PER SERVING: about 222 cal, 23 g pro, 10 g total fat (2 g sat. fat), 10 g carb, 2 g fibre, 81 mg chol, 383 mg sodium, 546 mg potassium. % RDI: 6% calcium, 14% iron, 9% vit A, 23% vit C, 10% folate.

Daniel's Favourite Pot Stickers

The Test Kitchen often takes inspiration from beloved family dishes. These tender pork dumplings were shared by food specialist Irene Fong, whose father, Daniel, always delights in them at family gatherings.

⅓ lb (150 g) **bok choy** (about 3 leaves), halved crosswise

1 lb (450 g) **lean ground pork**

1 tbsp **oyster sauce**

1 tsp **cornstarch**

1 tsp **soy sauce**

¼ tsp **pepper**

¼ tsp **sesame oil**

Pinch **salt**

1 **egg**, beaten

1 pkg (1 lb/450 g) **round dumpling wrappers**

2 tsp **vegetable oil**

In small pot of boiling lightly salted water, cook bok choy until tender, 4 to 5 minutes. Drain and let cool; squeeze out excess liquid. Thinly slice and place in large bowl. Mix in pork, oyster sauce, cornstarch, soy sauce, pepper, sesame oil, salt and half of the egg.

Mix 1 tsp water into remaining egg; brush over edge of 1 of the wrappers. Place rounded 1 tsp pork mixture in centre of wrapper. Fold over to match edges, pinching gently to seal and pressing lightly to flatten bottom.

Place, seam side up, on waxed paper–lined baking sheet; cover with damp towel. Repeat with remaining wrappers and filling. *(Make-ahead: Refrigerate, loosely covered with damp towel, in airtight container for up to 24 hours. Or freeze in single layer for 2 hours; transfer to airtight container and freeze for up to 3 weeks. Cook from frozen, adding ½ cup water and 4 minutes to cooking time.)*

In large nonstick skillet, in 2 batches, heat oil over medium-high heat; fry pot stickers, seam side up, until bottoms are light golden, about 1 minute. Pour in enough water to come ¼ inch (5 mm) up side of pan. Cover and reduce heat to medium; cook, without turning, until translucent and almost no liquid remains, 5 to 6 minutes.

Uncover and increase heat to medium-high; cook, turning to brown all sides, until no liquid remains, 5 to 6 minutes.

know your ingredients
Choosing Wrappers

Round dumpling wrappers are thicker than square wonton wrappers, but you can use either with delicious results.

Makes about 45 pieces. PER PIECE: about 50 cal, 3 g pro, 2 g total fat (1 g sat. fat), 5 g carb, trace fibre, 11 mg chol, 74 mg sodium, 52 mg potassium. % RDI: 1% calcium, 3% iron, 2% vit A, 2% vit C, 4% folate.

FREEZER
FRIENDLY

Spinach & Chicken Salad With Miso Vinaigrette

Light, fresh and appealing, a dinner salad like this is packed with nutrients, and it won't break the bank because it uses chicken thighs instead of breasts.

8 **boneless skinless chicken thighs**

Pinch each **salt** and **pepper**

1 bag (6 oz/170 g) **fresh baby spinach**

½ cup sliced **radishes**

MISO VINAIGRETTE:

2 tbsp **miso**

1 tbsp **granulated sugar**

1½ tsp **unseasoned rice vinegar**

1½ tsp **vegetable oil**

1 tsp **soy sauce**

1 tsp **sesame oil**

½ tsp minced **fresh ginger**

Trim any fat from chicken; sprinkle with salt and pepper. Place on greased grill over medium-high heat; close lid and grill, turning once, until lightly grill-marked and juices run clear when chicken is pierced, about 12 minutes.

MISO VINAIGRETTE: Meanwhile, in large bowl, whisk together miso, 2 tbsp water, sugar, vinegar, vegetable oil, soy sauce, sesame oil and ginger.

Slice chicken; add to vinaigrette. Add spinach and radishes; toss to coat.

change it up!

Spinach & Chicken Salad With Ginger Vinaigrette

Omit miso vinaigrette. In large bowl, whisk together 3 tbsp unseasoned rice vinegar, 2 tbsp vegetable oil, 1 tbsp water, 1 tsp each soy sauce and sesame oil, and ½ tsp each granulated sugar and minced fresh ginger. Toss with chicken, spinach and radishes as directed.

Makes 4 servings. PER SERVING: about 238 cal, 27 g pro, 11 g total fat (2 g sat. fat), 8 g carb, 2 g fibre, 95 mg chol, 525 mg sodium. % RDI: 6% calcium, 20% iron, 31% vit A, 25% vit C, 45% folate.

Mediterranean Pork & Vegetable Meat Loaf

Slice and serve hot with mashed potatoes or buttered orzo, or make delectable sandwiches with cold slices.

1 **onion**

1 **zucchini** (unpeeled)

1 tbsp **extra-virgin olive oil**

½ cup finely diced **sweet red pepper**

2 cloves **garlic,** minced

2 **eggs**

1 cup shredded **Fontina cheese**

⅔ cup **tomato sauce**

½ cup **fresh bread crumbs**

2 tsp **wine vinegar**

1 tsp **dried marjoram** or dried oregano

½ tsp each **salt** and **pepper**

¼ tsp **hot pepper flakes** (optional)

1¼ lb (565 g) **lean ground pork**

Coarsely grate onion and zucchini; squeeze out moisture.

In skillet, heat oil over medium heat; fry onion, zucchini, red pepper and garlic, stirring occasionally, until softened, about 10 minutes. Let cool.

Meanwhile, in large bowl, whisk together eggs, cheese, ¼ cup of the tomato sauce, bread crumbs, vinegar, marjoram, salt, pepper, and hot pepper flakes (if using); mix in pork and vegetable mixture. Pat evenly into 9- x 5-inch (2 L) loaf pan.

Bake in 350°F (180°C) oven until golden, 1 hour. Drain off fat; spread remaining tomato sauce over top. Bake until instant-read thermometer inserted into centre reads 160°F (71°C), about 30 minutes.

Makes 6 to 8 servings. PER EACH OF 8 SERVINGS: about 233 cal, 19 g pro, 15 g total fat (6 g sat. fat), 6 g carb, 1 g fibre, 108 mg chol, 431 mg sodium. % RDI: 10% calcium, 10% iron, 12% vit A, 30% vit C, 10% folate.

BACKYARD
BBQ FAVE

Maple Buttermilk Grilled Chicken

Using a mix of white and dark meat pieces gives diners the option to choose their favourite cuts. For a fun garnish, cut limes in half and grill alongside the chicken for the last 10 minutes – the warm juice is heavenly on grilled poultry.

2 cups **buttermilk**

2 **green onions,** chopped

4 cloves **garlic,** minced

½ tsp **pepper**

¼ tsp each **cinnamon** and **hot pepper flakes**

20 small **bone-in skin-on chicken pieces** (about 2½ lb/1.125 kg)

½ tsp **salt**

¼ cup **maple syrup**

In large bowl, stir together buttermilk, green onions, garlic, pepper, cinnamon and hot pepper flakes. Add chicken, turning to coat. Cover and refrigerate for 2 hours. *(Make-ahead: Refrigerate for up to 24 hours.)*

Remove chicken from marinade; discard marinade. Sprinkle chicken with salt. Place on greased grill over medium-high heat; close lid and grill, turning occasionally, until instant-read thermometer inserted into thickest part reads 165°F (74°C), about 35 minutes.

Grill, brushing with maple syrup, until glossy and coated, about 5 minutes.

how to

Coat Chicken Pieces Evenly

Be sure to cut chicken breasts in half crosswise, through the bone, to make them similar in size to the thighs and drumsticks. They'll cook more evenly that way.

Makes 10 to 12 servings. PER EACH OF 12 SERVINGS: about 113 cal, 10 g pro, 5 g total fat (2 g sat. fat), 6 g carb, trace fibre, 34 mg chol, 149 mg sodium, 157 mg potassium. % RDI: 3% calcium, 2% iron, 2% vit A, 2% folate.

Spice-Rubbed Pork Chops With Sweet & Sour Onion

Inexpensive and available everywhere, pork chops are a great option to cook throughout the year. The onion topping gives these chops a fresh tang.

1 tbsp packed **brown sugar**

1 tsp **smoked paprika**

½ tsp **garlic powder**

¼ tsp each **ground cumin, salt** and **pepper**

4 **boneless centre-cut pork chops** (1 lb/450 g total)

2 tsp **olive oil**

SWEET AND SOUR ONION:

1 tbsp **olive oil**

1 large **red onion,** thinly sliced

¼ cup **sherry vinegar**

2 tbsp **granulated sugar**

2 sprigs **fresh thyme**

Pinch each **salt** and **pepper**

SWEET AND SOUR ONION: In saucepan, heat oil over medium heat; cook onion, stirring occasionally, until softened, about 5 minutes. Add vinegar, sugar, thyme sprigs, salt and pepper; cook over medium-low heat until onion is caramelized, about 15 minutes. Discard thyme.

Meanwhile, combine brown sugar, paprika, garlic powder, cumin, salt and pepper; rub over both sides of pork chops.

In large skillet, heat oil over medium heat; cook pork chops, turning once, until juices run clear when pork is pierced and just a hint of pink remains inside, 6 to 8 minutes. Serve topped with sweet and sour onion.

Makes 4 servings. PER SERVING: about 292 cal, 24 g pro, 13 g total fat (3 g sat. fat), 19 g carb, 2 g fibre, 64 mg chol, 209 mg sodium, 493 mg potassium. % RDI: 4% calcium, 9% iron, 3% vit A, 10% vit C, 8% folate.

Slow Cooker Southern-Style Pork Roast

Pork shoulder is inexpensive and easy to find in grocery stores. Serve this roast alongside roasted potatoes or shred it with two forks to make pulled pork.

2 **onions,** thinly sliced

2 cloves **garlic,** minced

1 can (28 oz/796 mL) **diced tomatoes**

⅓ cup **cooking molasses**

¼ cup **cider vinegar**

3 tbsp packed **brown sugar**

2 tsp **chili powder**

1 tsp **salt**

½ tsp **pepper**

3 lb (1.35 kg) **boneless pork shoulder blade roast**

3 tbsp **all-purpose flour**

In slow cooker, combine onions, garlic, tomatoes, molasses, vinegar, brown sugar, chili powder, salt and pepper. Top with pork.

Cover and cook on low until pork is tender, 6 to 8 hours.

Transfer pork to platter; tent with foil and keep warm. Whisk flour with ¼ cup water until smooth; whisk into slow cooker. Cook, covered, on high until thickened slightly, about 30 minutes.

Separate pork into portions and serve with sauce.

Makes 8 servings. PER SERVING: about 316 cal, 22 g pro, 14 g total fat (5 g sat. fat), 26 g carb, 2 g fibre, 76 mg chol, 492 mg sodium, 767 mg potassium. % RDI: 8% calcium, 24% iron, 3% vit A, 25% vit C, 10% folate.

Pork Chops With Peppered Apples

Fast-fry pork chops are quick to prepare and let you throw together an impressive spread without blowing your budget. Serve with crusty bread.

8 **boneless fast-fry pork loin centre chops** (about 1 lb/450 g)

¼ tsp each **salt** and **pepper**

2 tsp **olive oil**

PEPPERED APPLES:

1 tbsp **butter**

3 **sweet-tart apples** (such as Cortland or Spartan), peeled and cut in ½-inch (1 cm) pieces

¼ cup **apple cider**

2 tsp **liquid honey**

¼ tsp **coarsely ground pepper**

Pinch **salt**

WARM CHARD SLAW:

2 tsp **olive oil**

2 cloves **garlic,** minced

2 tsp **liquid honey**

1 bunch **Swiss chard,** thinly sliced

2 tsp **lemon juice**

¼ tsp each **salt** and **pepper**

PEPPERED APPLES: In skillet, melt butter over medium-high heat; cook apples, stirring often, until tender-crisp, about 4 minutes. Stir in cider and honey; reduce heat to medium and cook, stirring occasionally, until apples are tender, about 5 minutes. Stir in pepper and salt. Set aside and keep warm.

Sprinkle both sides of pork chops with salt and pepper. In large skillet, heat oil over medium-high heat; cook chops, in batches and turning once, until juices run clear when pork is pierced and just a hint of pink remains inside, 4 to 6 minutes. Transfer to plate; keep warm.

WARM CHARD SLAW: In same skillet, heat oil over medium heat; cook garlic, stirring, for 30 seconds. Stir in honey until melted. Stir in chard; cook, stirring occasionally, until wilted, about 3 minutes. Stir in lemon juice, salt and pepper. Serve with pork chops and apples.

Makes 4 servings. PER SERVING: about 299 cal, 29 g pro, 10 g total fat (4 g sat. fat), 24 g carb, 3 g fibre, 67 mg chol, 509 mg sodium, 942 mg potassium. % RDI: 6% calcium, 23% iron, 50% vit A, 30% vit C, 5% folate.

Pork Chops With Puttanesca Sauce

A zesty caper- and olive-infused tomato sauce dolls up everyday pork chops.

2 tbsp **vegetable oil**

4 **pork loin centre chops** (boneless or bone-in), trimmed

1 **onion,** chopped

2 cloves **garlic,** minced

½ tsp each **pepper** and **hot pepper flakes**

¼ tsp **salt**

1 can (19 oz/540 mL) **whole tomatoes**

¼ cup **tomato paste**

½ cup chopped **Kalamata olives**

1 tbsp drained **capers**

¼ cup minced **fresh basil** or parsley

In large skillet, heat 1 tbsp of the oil over medium-high heat; brown pork chops. Transfer to plate.

Drain fat from pan; add remaining oil. Fry onion, garlic, pepper, hot pepper flakes and salt over medium heat until softened, about 4 minutes.

Add tomatoes and tomato paste; mash with potato masher. Add olives and capers; bring to boil, stirring and scraping up browned bits. Reduce heat and simmer until thickened, about 10 minutes.

Return pork and any accumulated juices to pan; add basil. Cover and simmer until juices run clear when pork is pierced and just a hint of pink remains inside, about 10 minutes.

Makes 4 servings. PER SERVING: about 292 cal, 25 g pro, 16 g total fat (2 g sat. fat), 14 g carb, 3 g fibre, 60 mg chol, 980 mg sodium. % RDI: 9% calcium, 19% iron, 14% vit A, 48% vit C, 10% folate.

Pork Piccata With Lemon Caper Sauce

Fast-fry pork topped with a flavourful sauce can be on the table in minutes. Serve with potatoes and sautéed rapini or broccoli.

8 **boneless fast-fry pork loin centre chops**

¼ cup **all-purpose flour**

¼ tsp each **salt** and **pepper**

3 tbsp **extra-virgin olive oil**

3 cloves **garlic,** minced

1 tbsp drained **capers**

½ cup **sodium-reduced chicken broth**

2 tbsp **lemon juice**

Between plastic wrap, pound pork to scant ¼-inch (5 mm) thickness. In plastic bag, combine flour, salt and pepper. One piece at a time, shake pork in flour mixture to coat.

In skillet, heat 1 tbsp of the oil over medium-high heat; cook pork, turning once, in 2 batches and adding more oil as necessary, until golden and just a hint of pink remains inside, about 3 minutes. Transfer to plate; keep warm.

Add remaining oil to pan; cook garlic and capers over medium heat for 1 minute.

Add broth and lemon juice; boil for 1 minute. Serve with pork.

Makes 4 servings. PER SERVING: about 302 cal, 6 g pro, 18 g total fat (4 g sat. fat), 7 g carb, trace fibre, 73 mg chol, 357 mg sodium. % RDI: 3% calcium, 10% iron, 5% vit C, 7% folate.

CANADIAN
CLASSIC

Easy Tourtière

This simplified version of the French-Canadian classic doesn't require mashed potatoes and has a super-flaky crust that will prompt everyone to ask for the recipe.

1 pkg (8 oz/225 g) **button mushrooms,** trimmed

1 small **onion,** quartered

2 cloves **garlic**

2 tsp **vegetable oil**

1½ lb (675 g) **lean ground pork**

2 tbsp **quick-cooking rolled oats**

¾ tsp each **salt** and **pepper**

½ tsp each **dried thyme** and **savory**

¼ tsp **ground cloves**

1 **egg,** beaten

REALLY FLAKY PASTRY:

3 cups **all-purpose flour**

1 tsp **salt**

½ cup each cold **unsalted butter** and **lard,** cubed

1 **egg**

2 tsp **vinegar**

Ice water

how to

Make a Flaky Crust

For the flakiest pastry, make sure you're working with cold butter and lard and don't overwork the dough.

In food processor, pulse mushrooms, onion and garlic until finely chopped. In nonstick skillet, heat oil over medium-high heat; cook onion mixture, stirring, until no liquid remains, 5 minutes. Transfer to bowl. In same pan, brown pork, breaking up with spoon, 8 minutes. Stir in oats, salt, pepper, thyme, savory and cloves. Stir in onion mixture and ⅓ cup water; cook over medium-low heat, uncovered and stirring, until almost no liquid remains, 10 minutes. Transfer to bowl. Cover; refrigerate for 45 minutes. *(Make-ahead: Refrigerate for up to 24 hours.)*

REALLY FLAKY PASTRY: Meanwhile, in bowl, whisk flour with salt. Using pastry blender, cut in butter and lard until in coarse crumbs with a few larger pieces. In liquid measure, beat egg with vinegar; add enough ice water to make ⅔ cup. Drizzle over flour mixture, tossing with fork until ragged dough forms. Divide in half; press into discs. Wrap each and refrigerate until chilled, about 30 minutes. *(Make-ahead: Refrigerate for up to 2 days.)*

Mix egg with 1 tbsp water. On floured surface, roll out 1 disc to scant ¼-inch (5 mm) thickness; fit into 9-inch (23 cm) pie plate. Spoon in filling. Roll out remaining pastry. Brush pie rim with egg; cover with pastry. Trim, leaving ¾-inch (2 cm) overhang. Fold overhang under rim; press to seal. *(Make-ahead: Cover and refrigerate for up to 24 hours.)*

Brush top with egg; cut steam vents in top. Bake in bottom third of 400°F (200°C) oven until golden, 50 minutes. Let stand for 10 minutes before serving.

Makes 8 servings. PER SERVING: about 579 cal, 23 g pro, 38 g total fat (17 g sat. fat), 35 g carb, 2 g fibre, 137 mg chol, 546 mg sodium, 412 mg potassium. % RDI: 3% calcium, 25% iron, 11% vit A, 3% vit C, 45% folate.

Sweet Chili Chicken

Warm and comforting, this sweet and spicy chicken is best served with plain steamed rice accompanied by stir-fried broccoli or bok choy.

1½ lb (675 g) **boneless skinless chicken thighs,** cut in bite-size pieces

¼ tsp **salt**

1 tbsp **vegetable oil**

1 clove **garlic,** minced

2 tsp finely chopped **fresh ginger**

1 **onion,** chopped

1 each **sweet red pepper** and **sweet green pepper,** cut in bite-size pieces

1 **jalapeño pepper,** seeded and finely chopped

½ cup **Thai-style sweet chili sauce**

1 tbsp **unseasoned rice vinegar**

2 **green onions,** thinly sliced

Sprinkle chicken with salt. In large skillet, heat oil over high heat; stir-fry chicken until starting to brown and juices run clear when chicken is pierced, about 6 minutes.

Add garlic and ginger; stir-fry until fragrant, about 1 minute. Add onion, red and green peppers and jalapeño pepper; stir-fry for 3 minutes, adding about 4 tbsp water, 1 tbsp at a time, to prevent mixture from sticking to pan.

Mix chili sauce with vinegar; add to pan and cook over medium-high heat, stirring often, until reduced and vegetables are tender-crisp. Serve sprinkled with green onions.

Makes 6 servings. PER SERVING: about 227 cal, 23 g pro, 8 g total fat (2 g sat. fat), 13 g carb, 1 g fibre, 94 mg chol, 355 mg sodium, 378 mg potassium. % RDI: 2% calcium, 11% iron, 10% vit A, 87% vit C, 9% folate.

Black Bean, Ground Pork & Green Bean Stir-Fry

Once the prep is done, this simple weeknight stir-fry comes together in a flash.

3 tbsp **black bean sauce**

1 tbsp **cornstarch**

1 tbsp **unseasoned rice vinegar**

Pinch **granulated sugar**

2 tbsp **vegetable oil**

1 lb (450 g) **lean ground pork**

3 **green onions,** sliced (white and green parts separated)

1 tbsp minced **fresh ginger**

6 oz (170 g) **green beans,** trimmed and cut in 1-inch (2.5 cm) lengths

Whisk together black bean sauce, cornstarch, vinegar, sugar and ½ cup water; set aside.

In wok, heat 1 tbsp of the oil over medium-high heat; stir-fry pork until no longer pink, about 3 minutes. Drain off fat; set pork aside.

Add remaining oil to wok; stir-fry white parts of green onions and ginger for 30 seconds. Add green beans; stir-fry for 2 minutes.

Add pork and black bean mixture; stir-fry for 2 minutes. Add green parts of green onions; stir-fry for 1 minute.

Makes 4 servings. PER SERVING: about 328 cal, 23 g pro, 20 g total fat (6 g sat. fat), 11 g carb, 2 g fibre, 66 mg chol, 194 mg sodium, 522 mg potassium. % RDI: 4% calcium, 16% iron, 4% vit A, 10% vit C, 10% folate.

Chicken With Noodles, Shiitake Mushrooms & Snow Peas

Linguine is a good (even cheaper) substitute for udon noodles; just cook the pasta for two minutes less than the package directions indicate.

1 tbsp **vegetable oil**

1 lb (450 g) **boneless skinless chicken thighs,** thinly sliced

2 tsp each minced **garlic** and **fresh ginger**

2 cups **shiitake mushroom caps,** thinly sliced

¼ cup **hoisin sauce**

1 tbsp **oyster sauce**

1 tsp **sambal oelek** or hot sauce

4 pkg (7 oz/200 g each) **fresh udon noodles**

1 cup **snow peas,** thinly sliced lengthwise

1 tsp **sesame oil**

In wok or large skillet, heat vegetable oil over medium-high heat; stir-fry chicken, garlic and ginger until chicken is lightly browned, about 5 minutes.

Add mushrooms; stir-fry until beginning to soften, about 2 minutes. Stir in ½ cup water, hoisin sauce, oyster sauce and sambal oelek; bring to simmer.

Add noodles and toss to combine; simmer until sauce is thickened, 2 to 3 minutes. Add snow peas and sesame oil; cook for 1 minute.

Makes 4 servings. PER SERVING: about 809 cal, 38 g pro, 14 g total fat (3 g sat. fat), 125 g carb, 3 g fibre, 95 mg chol, 738 mg sodium, 467 mg potassium. % RDI: 6% calcium, 21% iron, 4% vit A, 18% vit C, 9% folate.

BETTER
THAN
TAKEOUT!

Hungarian Bean
Soup, page 111

chapter three

Eggs, Beans & Tofu

Kale, Bean & Sausage Soup

Kale is rich in nutrients and adds a wonderful fresh note to this 30-minute bean and sausage soup. Serve it with bread to soak up the delicious broth.

2 tbsp **olive oil**

1 **Spanish onion,** sliced

2 cloves **garlic,** minced

1 large **baking potato,** peeled and cubed

1 **bay leaf**

½ tsp **sweet paprika**

¼ tsp each **salt** and **pepper**

6 cups chopped stemmed **kale** (about half bunch)

1 can (19 oz/540 mL) **white kidney beans,** drained and rinsed

8 oz (225 g) **summer sausage,** cubed

In large Dutch oven, heat half of the oil over medium heat; cook onion and garlic, stirring occasionally, until softened, 4 to 5 minutes.

Add potato, bay leaf and paprika; cook, stirring, for 1 minute.

Add 4 cups water, salt and pepper; bring to boil. Reduce heat, cover and simmer until potato is tender-firm, about 10 minutes.

Add kale and beans; simmer until kale is tender, 5 to 7 minutes. Discard bay leaf.

Meanwhile, in skillet, heat remaining oil over medium-high heat; fry sausage until browned. Sprinkle over bowlfuls of soup to serve.

Makes 4 servings. PER SERVING: about 497 cal, 19 g pro, 25 g total fat (7 g sat. fat), 54 g carb, 13 g fibre, 39 mg chol, 900 mg sodium, 1,208 mg potassium. % RDI: 20% calcium, 29% iron, 141% vit A, 192% vit C, 38% folate.

READY IN
30 MINUTES

Hearty Tomato, Sausage & Bean Soup

For a fancier finish, garnish this Italian-inspired soup with shavings of Parmesan cheese or drizzle with a touch of extra-virgin olive oil.

4 tsp **vegetable oil**

1 **onion,** finely chopped

1 each **carrot** and rib **celery,** finely chopped

2 cloves **garlic,** minced

1 **green finger hot pepper** (optional)

¼ tsp each **salt** and **pepper**

2 **mild Italian sausages** (8 oz/ 225 g total), casings removed

2 cans (28 oz/796 mL each) **whole tomatoes**

1 can (19 oz/540 mL) **navy beans,** drained and rinsed

1 cup **sodium-reduced chicken broth**

⅓ cup chopped **fresh oregano**

1 tsp **granulated sugar**

In Dutch oven, heat oil over medium heat; cook onion, carrot, celery, garlic, hot pepper (if using), salt and pepper, stirring occasionally, until softened, about 6 minutes.

Increase heat to medium-high; add sausage meat and cook, breaking up with spoon, for 5 minutes.

Stir in tomatoes, breaking up with spoon. Add beans, broth, 1 cup water, oregano and sugar; bring to boil. Reduce heat and simmer until slightly thickened, 15 to 20 minutes. Discard hot pepper.

change it up!

Spicy Hearty Tomato, Sausage & Bean Soup

Substitute hot Italian sausages for the mild and increase the green finger hot pepper to taste.

Makes 8 to 10 servings. PER EACH OF 10 SERVINGS: about 171 cal, 9 g pro, 8 g total fat (2 g sat. fat), 19 g carb, 3 g fibre, 12 mg chol, 647 mg sodium, 526 mg potassium. % RDI: 8% calcium, 21% iron, 15% vit A, 38% vit C, 17% folate.

Hungarian Bean Soup

Hearty, warming and tasty – what more could you ask for in a soup? Whisk in ½ cup sour cream at the end or serve some at the table for a creamy variation.

1½ cups **dried red kidney beans**

2 tbsp **vegetable oil**

⅔ lb (300 g) **kielbasa sausage,** sliced

2 **onions,** diced

4 cloves **garlic,** minced

2 tbsp **tomato paste**

4 tsp **sweet paprika**

1 **bay leaf**

2 each **carrots** and ribs **celery,** sliced

¾ tsp **salt**

Rinse and soak beans overnight in 3 times their volume of water. (Or bring to boil and boil gently for 2 minutes. Remove from heat, cover and let stand for 1 hour.) Drain.

In Dutch oven, heat half of the oil over medium-high heat; cook kielbasa, stirring occasionally, until browned, about 5 minutes. With slotted spoon, transfer to paper towel–lined plate; set aside.

Heat remaining oil in pan over medium heat; cook onions and garlic until softened, about 6 minutes. Stir in tomato paste and paprika; cook, stirring, for 1 minute.

Add beans, kielbasa, 9 cups water and bay leaf; bring to boil. Skim off any foam. Reduce heat, cover and simmer until beans are tender, about 45 minutes.

Stir in carrots, celery and salt; simmer until tender, about 15 minutes. Discard bay leaf.

Makes 8 servings. PER SERVING: about 258 cal, 15 g pro, 10 g total fat (2 g sat. fat), 28 g carb, 8 g fibre, 25 mg chol, 597 mg sodium. % RDI: 6% calcium, 27% iron, 38% vit A, 7% vit C, 60% folate.

Chana Masala

This is India's answer to vegetarian comfort food. If you like heat, add a finely chopped red hot pepper or two with the garlic. Garnish with a dab of plain yogurt.

3 tbsp **olive oil**

2 **onions,** chopped

6 cloves **garlic,** minced

2 tbsp grated **fresh ginger**

2 tsp each **chili powder, ground coriander, ground cumin** and **garam masala**

2 cans (19 oz/540 mL each) **chickpeas,** drained and rinsed

½ cup **tomato paste**

2 tsp packed **brown sugar**

¼ tsp **salt**

2 tbsp **lemon juice**

In saucepan, heat oil over medium-high heat; cook onions, stirring occasionally, until softened, about 5 minutes.

Add garlic and ginger; cook for 1 minute. Stir in chili powder, coriander, cumin and garam masala; cook until fragrant, about 1 minute.

Stir in chickpeas, 1 cup water, tomato paste, brown sugar and salt, scraping up any browned bits. Reduce heat, cover and simmer until slightly thickened, about 15 minutes. Stir in lemon juice.

Makes 4 servings. PER SERVING: about 439 cal, 14 g pro, 14 g total fat (2 g sat. fat), 69 g carb, 14 g fibre, 0 mg chol, 778 mg sodium, 870 mg potassium. % RDI: 11% calcium, 38% iron, 9% vit A, 35% vit C, 65% folate.

Black Bean Rice Bowl

Beans and rice are a vegetarian one-dish combination enjoyed around the world. Serve this flavourful rice bowl with lime wedges to squeeze over top.

1 cup **long-grain white rice**

½ tsp **salt**

1 tbsp **chili powder**

¼ tsp each **ground cumin, ground coriander** and **dried oregano**

¼ tsp **pepper**

1 tbsp **vegetable oil**

½ cup diced **red onion**

3 **green onions** (white and light green parts only), sliced

3 cloves **garlic,** minced

1 can (19 oz/540 mL) **black beans,** drained and rinsed

¾ cup **frozen corn kernels**

1 tbsp **lime juice**

1 small **avocado,** pitted, peeled and diced

1 **plum tomato,** diced

¼ cup chopped **fresh cilantro**

In small saucepan, combine 1½ cups water, rice and ¼ tsp of the salt; bring to boil. Reduce heat, cover and simmer until rice is tender and no liquid remains, about 10 minutes. Turn off heat; let stand on burner for 5 minutes. Fluff with fork.

Meanwhile, stir together chili powder, cumin, coriander, oregano, pepper and remaining salt; set aside.

In large skillet, heat oil over medium heat; cook red onion and green onions, stirring occasionally, until slightly softened, about 2 minutes. Stir in chili powder mixture and garlic; cook, stirring, for 1 minute.

Add black beans, corn and 1 cup water; bring to boil. Reduce heat and simmer until almost no liquid remains and corn is heated through, about 3 minutes. Stir in lime juice.

Divide rice among bowls; top with bean mixture, avocado, tomato and cilantro.

change it up!

Black Bean & Chicken Rice Bowl

Cook rice as directed. Toss together 6 boneless skinless chicken thighs, 2 tsp lime juice and 1 tsp of the chili powder mixture. In large skillet, heat 2 tsp vegetable oil over medium heat; cook chicken, turning once, until juices run clear when thickest part is pierced, about 12 minutes. Cut into bite-size pieces. Meanwhile, cook bean mixture as directed. Top rice with chicken and bean mixture; garnish as directed.

Makes 4 servings. PER SERVING: about 399 cal, 12 g pro, 10 g total fat (1 g sat. fat), 68 g carb, 12 g fibre, 0 mg chol, 672 mg sodium, 721 mg potassium. % RDI: 7% calcium, 22% iron, 10% vit A, 22% vit C, 45% folate.

Quick Lentil Curry

All varieties of lentils cook quickly and taste great, so they're a handy pantry ingredient. Serve this curry over rice with a steamed vegetable or sautéed greens. For a delicious vegan dish, simply omit the fried eggs.

2 tbsp **vegetable oil**

1 **onion,** finely chopped

1 clove **garlic,** pressed

2 tsp grated **fresh ginger**

1 finger-size strip seeded **red finger hot pepper** or green finger hot pepper

1½ tsp **garam masala**

½ tsp **salt**

¼ tsp **turmeric**

1 cup **dried green lentils**

1 cup halved **grape tomatoes**

2 tbsp chopped **fresh cilantro**

1 tsp **lemon juice**

EGGS:

2 tsp **vegetable oil**

4 **eggs**

In saucepan, heat oil over medium-high heat; cook onion, stirring, until golden, about 2 minutes. Stir in garlic, ginger, hot pepper, garam masala, salt and turmeric; cook, stirring, for 30 seconds. Add ¼ cup water; cook, stirring, until thick paste forms, about 2 minutes.

Stir in lentils and 2½ cups water; bring to boil. Reduce heat, cover and simmer, stirring often, until lentils are tender and almost no liquid remains, 35 to 40 minutes. Stir in tomatoes, cilantro and lemon juice.

EGGS: In large skillet, heat oil over medium-high heat; fry eggs, turning once, until whites are set but yolks are still runny, 2 to 3 minutes. Serve with lentil mixture.

time-saver

Use Canned Instead of Dried

Substitute 1 can (19 oz/540 mL) lentils, drained and rinsed, for the dried lentils. Decrease the water to 1½ cups and cooking time to 20 minutes.

Makes 4 servings. PER SERVING: about 337 cal, 19 g pro, 15 g total fat (2 g sat. fat), 34 g carb, 7 g fibre, 186 mg chol, 354 mg sodium, 718 mg potassium. % RDI: 6% calcium, 41% iron, 10% vit A, 12% vit C, 129% folate.

Slow Cooker Chickpea & Squash Curry

Curries like this vegetarian one are terrific made in the slow cooker. Serve with basmati rice or naan for a simple, complete family-style feast.

1 tbsp **vegetable oil**

1 large **onion,** chopped

2 cloves **garlic,** minced

1 tbsp minced **fresh ginger**

1 **green finger hot pepper,** minced

4 tsp **garam masala**

1 tsp **turmeric**

1 tsp **cumin seeds,** crushed

½ tsp **salt**

¼ tsp **pepper**

6 **plum tomatoes,** chopped

2 cans (19 oz/540 mL each) **chickpeas,** drained and rinsed

1 **butternut squash** (2½ lb/1.125 kg), peeled and cut in 1-inch (2.5 cm) chunks

2 tbsp chopped **fresh cilantro**

1 tbsp **lemon juice**

RAITA:

2 cups **Balkan-style plain yogurt**

1 cup grated peeled **cucumber,** squeezed and patted dry

2 tbsp each minced **fresh mint** and **fresh cilantro**

1 tbsp **lemon juice**

1 tsp **cumin seeds,** crushed

Pinch each **salt** and **pepper**

In large skillet, heat oil over medium heat; cook onion, stirring occasionally, until softened, about 5 minutes.

Stir in garlic, ginger and hot pepper; cook for 2 minutes. Stir in garam masala, turmeric, cumin seeds, salt and pepper; cook for 2 minutes. Add tomatoes and ⅓ cup water; cook, stirring, for 2 minutes, scraping up browned bits. Pour into slow cooker.

Stir chickpeas and squash into slow cooker. Cover and cook on low until squash is tender, 3 to 4 hours. Stir in cilantro and lemon juice.

RAITA: Meanwhile, in cheesecloth-lined strainer set over bowl, drain yogurt for 1 hour; discard liquid. Mix together drained yogurt, cucumber, mint, cilantro, lemon juice, cumin seeds, salt and pepper. Serve with curry.

Makes 8 servings. PER SERVING: about 280 cal, 10 g pro, 7 g total fat (3 g sat. fat), 47 g carb, 8 g fibre, 10 mg chol, 463 mg sodium, 795 mg potassium. % RDI: 17% calcium, 24% iron, 138% vit A, 52% vit C, 46% folate.

Jalapeño Bean Cakes With Lime Mayo

These tasty little cakes are a breeze to make with a food processor. To complete the meal, serve with a side salad or with coleslaw dressed with a light vinaigrette.

1 clove **garlic**

4 **green onions,** chopped

1 **jalapeño pepper,** seeded and chopped

1 can (19 oz/540 mL) **white kidney beans,** drained and rinsed

¾ cup **fresh bread crumbs**

¼ cup chopped **fresh parsley**

¼ tsp **pepper**

Pinch **salt**

1 **egg**

¼ cup **cornmeal**

1 tbsp **olive oil**

⅓ cup **light mayonnaise**

1 tsp **lime juice**

In food processor, pulse together garlic, green onions and jalapeño pepper until finely chopped. Add beans, bread crumbs, parsley, pepper, salt and egg; pulse until combined, leaving pieces of beans. Form into eight 2-inch (5 cm) patties. Gently dredge in cornmeal; refrigerate in single layer for 10 minutes.

In large nonstick skillet, heat oil over medium heat; cook patties, turning once, until golden, 8 to 10 minutes. Meanwhile, stir mayonnaise with lime juice. Serve with bean cakes.

change it up!

Chipotle Bean Cakes With Lime Mayo
Replace jalapeño pepper with 1 canned chipotle pepper in adobo sauce and 1 tsp adobo sauce; replace fresh parsley with fresh cilantro.

Makes 4 servings. PER SERVING: about 273 cal, 10 g pro, 13 g total fat (2 g sat. fat), 32 g carb, 9 g fibre, 54 mg chol, 504 mg sodium, 367 mg potassium. % RDI: 6% calcium, 16% iron, 7% vit A, 15% vit C, 35% folate.

Spanish Tortilla

This delicious thick "cake" of fried potatoes, eggs and onions is similar to a frittata. Save any leftovers and sandwich them in bread for lunch the next day.

2 **potatoes** (about 1 lb/450 g)

3 tbsp **vegetable oil**

2 **onions,** thinly sliced

2 cloves **garlic,** minced

½ tsp **salt**

¼ tsp **pepper**

Pinch **cayenne pepper**

6 **eggs,** beaten

Peel potatoes. Cut in half lengthwise; thinly slice crosswise.

In 10-inch (25 cm) ovenproof nonstick skillet, heat oil over medium-high heat; cook potatoes, onions, garlic, salt, pepper and cayenne pepper, stirring occasionally, until potatoes are tender and onions are light golden, about 20 minutes.

Smooth top. Pour eggs over potato mixture; cook over medium-low heat until set around edge, about 20 minutes.

Broil, about 6 inches (15 cm) from heat, until golden and eggs are completely set, about 2 minutes. Loosen edge. Let stand for 3 minutes. Invert onto plate; invert again onto another plate, top side up. *(Make-ahead: Let cool for 30 minutes. Refrigerate in airtight container for up to 2 days.)*

Makes 6 to 8 servings. PER EACH OF 8 SERVINGS: about 151 cal, 6 g pro, 9 g total fat (2 g sat. fat), 12 g carb, 1 g fibre, 140 mg chol, 192 mg sodium. % RDI: 3% calcium, 4% iron, 5% vit A, 7% vit C, 12% folate.

EASY
VEGAN

Curried Cauliflower With Chickpeas

This savoury dish has a little heat and a touch of sweetness from the raisins and caramelized onions. Serve with basmati rice.

1 tbsp **olive oil**

1 **sweet onion** (such as Vidalia), thinly sliced

1 tbsp **granulated sugar**

2 tbsp minced **fresh ginger**

2 cloves **garlic,** thinly sliced

2 tsp **garam masala**

2 tsp **balsamic vinegar**

¼ tsp **cayenne pepper**

¼ tsp each **salt** and **pepper**

1 small head **cauliflower**

1 can (19 oz/540 mL) **chickpeas,** drained and rinsed

¼ cup **raisins**

4 cups packed **fresh baby spinach**

In Dutch oven, heat oil over medium-high heat; cook onion and sugar, stirring occasionally, until beginning to brown, about 6 minutes.

Add ginger, garlic, garam masala, vinegar, cayenne pepper, salt and pepper; reduce heat to medium-low and cook, stirring occasionally, until onion is deep golden, 8 to 10 minutes.

Meanwhile, cut cauliflower into florets to make 6 cups. Add to pan along with chickpeas, raisins and ¼ cup water; cover and cook, stirring once or twice, until cauliflower is tender, about 18 minutes.

Remove from heat. Stir in spinach.

Makes 4 servings. PER SERVING: about 284 cal, 10 g pro, 6 g total fat (1 g sat. fat), 52 g carb, 11 g fibre, 0 mg chol, 487 mg sodium, 736 mg potassium. % RDI: 11% calcium, 27% iron, 31% vit A, 127% vit C, 85% folate.

Vegetarian Burgers

Everyone loves a good veggie burger. And this one is a simple, delicious rendition you can make at home when you want an alternative to meat.

⅔ cup **quick-cooking rolled oats** (not instant)

3 tbsp **vegetable oil**

1 **onion,** diced

2 cloves **garlic,** chopped

1 tsp **dried thyme**

¼ tsp each **salt** and **pepper**

1 **egg**

4 tsp **Dijon mustard**

1 pkg (340 g) **precooked ground soy protein mixture** (such as Yves Veggie Ground Round)

½ cup **mayonnaise**

4 **hamburger buns**

4 leaves **leaf lettuce**

8 slices **tomato**

4 slices **Swiss cheese** (optional)

In large skillet, toast oats over medium-high heat, stirring, until golden, about 3 minutes. Transfer to food processor; pulse until coarsely powdered.

In same skillet, heat 1 tbsp of the oil; cook onion, garlic, thyme, salt and pepper, stirring occasionally, until light golden, about 4 minutes. Add to food processor along with egg and half of the mustard; pulse until combined. Transfer to bowl; stir in ground soy; shape into 4 patties.

In skillet, heat remaining oil over medium heat; cook patties, turning once, until crisp and golden, 8 to 10 minutes.

Stir mayonnaise with remaining mustard; spread over buns. Sandwich lettuce, tomato, patties, and cheese (if using) in buns.

Makes 4 servings. PER SERVING: about 626 cal, 26 g pro, 37 g total fat (5 g sat. fat), 48 g carb, 9 g fibre, 57 mg chol, 1,042 mg sodium, 686 mg potassium. % RDI: 16% calcium, 54% iron, 10% vit A, 15% vit C, 38% folate.

Couscous Salad With Lentils & Dates

Whole wheat couscous is a quick-to-prepare base for this mildly spiced salad.

¾ cup **whole wheat couscous**

1 tsp grated **orange zest**

½ tsp **ground cumin**

¼ tsp **cinnamon**

Half **sweet red pepper,** finely diced

1 cup rinsed drained **canned lentils**

½ cup chopped **dates** (or ¼ cup dried currants)

¼ cup **toasted slivered almonds**

2 tbsp chopped **fresh parsley**

DRESSING:

2 tbsp **extra-virgin olive oil**

2 tbsp **orange juice**

2 tsp **white wine vinegar**

1 tsp **Dijon mustard**

½ tsp **salt**

In large bowl, combine couscous, orange zest, cumin and cinnamon. Add 1¼ cups boiling water; cover and let stand for 5 minutes. Fluff with fork; let cool.

Add red pepper, lentils and dates; toss to combine.

DRESSING: Whisk together oil, orange juice, vinegar, mustard and salt; pour over couscous mixture and toss gently to coat. *(Make-ahead: Cover and refrigerate for up to 24 hours.)*

Sprinkle with almonds and parsley.

Makes 4 servings. PER SERVING: about 367 cal, 12 g pro, 12 g total fat (1 g sat. fat), 59 g carb, 10 g fibre, 0 mg chol, 429 mg sodium. % RDI: 5% calcium, 27% iron, 10% vit A, 60% vit C, 47% folate.

Budget-Friendly Beans & Tofu

What Makes Them Affordable:
Whether you call them beans or pulses, the dried seeds of plants in the legume family are one of the smartest budget ingredients you can include in your diet. Legumes produce abundant, protein-packed seeds and require only a fraction of the energy and water needed to raise animals for meat.

You can store dried beans almost indefinitely, meaning there's little worry about waste. Canned beans and lentils are more expensive than their dried counterparts, but are still fairly cheap and save quite a bit of prep time.

Tofu and many other meat substitutes are made from soybeans, another nutritious member of the legume family. Like whole legumes, these derivatives contain protein that costs less to produce than a comparable amount of meat protein.

Why They're Good for You: Beans and lentils are low in fat and high in healthy soluble fibre and protein. They're also sources of folate, zinc, phosphorus, iron and B vitamins. Canned beans are high in salt, so rinse them well before adding them to recipes, or use no-salt-added versions.

Tofu is higher in fat than dried beans, but it contains healthy unsaturated fat. Tofu and other foods made from whole soybeans also contain isoflavones, which are thought to protect against certain cancers.

Food Safety: Dried beans will keep almost indefinitely. Seal them in an airtight container (a large canning jar is ideal) and keep them in a cool, dry corner of the kitchen or pantry. Canned beans, like all canned goods, should last for a couple of years – check the label for a best-by date to be sure. Tofu and soy products, such as ground soy protein and tempeh, should reside in the refrigerator. Once opened, tofu doesn't last long. If you have part of a block left over, place it in an airtight container and cover with fresh water (preferably filtered) and keep for only a day or two longer.

Uses: Beans and lentils are often the stars in soups, stews and curries. They also make wonderful salads – especially lentils and chickpeas. Tofu is bland on its own but readily soaks up the flavours around it. Try it in stir-fries, on the grill or roasted, and always pair it with a well-spiced, savoury sauce to enhance its delicate flavour.

Panzanella Salad With Poached Eggs

Don't throw away a stale loaf of bread. Do as the Tuscans do and celebrate with a bread salad – it's an old-fashioned, frugal light dinner.

4 cups cubed (1 inch/2.5 cm) crustless **Italian loaf** or **French loaf**

⅓ cup **extra-virgin olive oil**

3 tbsp **red wine vinegar**

4 **anchovy fillets,** finely chopped

2 **shallots,** thinly sliced

2 cloves **garlic,** minced

1 tbsp drained **capers**

Pinch each **salt** and **pepper**

2 cups halved **cherry tomatoes**

2 cups cubed (1 inch/2.5 cm) **English cucumber**

¼ cup chopped **fresh basil**

4 **eggs,** poached (see How-To, below)

Spread bread on baking sheet; drizzle with 2 tbsp of the oil. Bake in 350°F (180°C) oven, stirring once, until golden and crisp, about 15 minutes. Let cool.

In large bowl, whisk together remaining oil, vinegar, anchovies, shallots, garlic, capers, salt and pepper. Add tomatoes, cucumber, basil and croutons; toss to coat. Serve topped with eggs.

how-to

Perfect Poached Eggs

In large saucepan or deep skillet, heat 2 to 3 inches (5 to 8 cm) water with 1 tsp vinegar over medium heat until simmering. One at a time, crack eggs into small bowl; gently slide into simmering water. Poach until white is set and yolk is soft, about 3 minutes.

Makes 4 servings. PER SERVING: about 353 cal, 11 g pro, 25 g total fat (4 g sat. fat), 22 g carb, 2 g fibre, 190 mg chol, 455 mg sodium, 418 mg potassium. % RDI: 8% calcium, 17% iron, 16% vit A, 22% vit C, 38% folate.

LEFTOVER
BUSTER

Bean, Mushroom & Wilted Spinach Salad

Warm and satisfying, this supper salad is filling and packed with healthy fibre.

8 oz (225 g) **yellow beans** or green beans, trimmed

1 bag (6 oz/170 g) **fresh baby spinach**

3 tbsp **extra-virgin olive oil**

1 small **sweet onion,** thinly sliced

8 oz (225 g) **cremini mushrooms**

1 clove **garlic,** minced

¼ tsp each **salt, pepper** and **dried thyme**

1 cup rinsed drained **canned chickpeas**

3 tbsp **white wine vinegar**

4 **hard-cooked eggs** (see How-To, page 237), quartered

3 tbsp shaved **Asiago cheese**

In saucepan of boiling water, blanch beans until tender-crisp, about 2 minutes. Drain and set aside.

Meanwhile, place spinach in large bowl; set aside.

In large skillet, heat oil over medium-high heat; sauté onion until tender, about 5 minutes.

Add mushrooms, garlic, salt, pepper and thyme; cook until mushrooms are tender and golden, about 7 minutes.

Add blanched beans, chickpeas and vinegar; cook until heated through. Add to spinach; toss until wilted and coated.

Arrange salad on plates. Top with eggs; sprinkle with cheese.

Makes 4 servings. PER SERVING: about 352 cal, 18 g pro, 18 g total fat (4 g sat. fat), 32 g carb, 10 g fibre, 190 mg chol, 530 mg sodium, 814 mg potassium. % RDI: 18% calcium, 31% iron, 51% vit A, 15% vit C, 76% folate.

Chickpea Salad With Lemon Cumin Vinaigrette

Bean salads are great for dinner, and leftovers make a simple lunch the next day.

2 **pitas** (with pockets)

1 can (19 oz/540 mL) **chickpeas,** drained and rinsed

3 **plum tomatoes,** chopped

1 cup chopped **English cucumber**

1 cup chopped **sweet green pepper**

3 **green onions,** thinly sliced

½ cup chopped **walnuts**

¼ cup chopped **fresh mint** (or 1 tsp dried)

8 leaves Boston, Bibb or leaf **lettuce**

⅓ cup crumbled **feta cheese**

VINAIGRETTE:

3 tbsp **lemon juice**

2 tbsp **extra-virgin olive oil**

2 tsp **ground cumin**

¾ tsp **salt**

¼ tsp **cayenne pepper**

Toast pitas; cut each into 8 wedges.

VINAIGRETTE: In large bowl, whisk together lemon juice, oil, cumin, salt and cayenne pepper.

Add chickpeas, tomatoes, cucumber, green pepper, green onions, walnuts and mint to bowl; toss to coat.

Line 4 individual salad bowls with 2 lettuce leaves each; spoon chickpea salad into lettuce. Sprinkle with feta cheese. Serve with pita wedges.

Makes 4 servings. PER SERVING: about 430 cal, 13 g pro, 21 g total fat (4 g sat. fat), 52 g carb, 8 g fibre, 9 mg chol, 997 mg sodium. % RDI: 15% calcium, 31% iron, 11% vit A, 90% vit C, 64% folate.

Grilled Peanut Tofu Salad

Grilled tofu has a nice, crispy crust that's especially good topped with a savoury peanut sauce. This is a beautiful, light main dish if you're entertaining.

⅓ cup **natural peanut butter**

¼ cup **lime juice**

2 cloves **garlic,** minced

2 tbsp each **liquid honey** and **soy sauce**

½ tsp each **salt** and **pepper**

1 pkg (1 lb/454 g) **firm tofu,** drained

1 tbsp **vegetable oil**

8 cups torn **leaf lettuce**

2 cups shredded **carrots**

1 cup **bean sprouts**

2 **green onions,** thinly sliced

¼ cup chopped **roasted peanuts**

In bowl, whisk together peanut butter, lime juice, garlic, 2 tbsp hot water, honey, soy sauce and half each of the salt and pepper.

Cut tofu horizontally into 4 slices; pat dry. Brush with oil; sprinkle with remaining salt and pepper. Place on greased grill over medium-high heat; close lid and grill, turning once, until grill-marked, about 10 minutes. Cut each into quarters.

Arrange lettuce on 4 plates. Top each with 4 pieces of the tofu, carrots, then bean sprouts. Drizzle with dressing; sprinkle with green onions and peanuts.

Makes 4 servings. PER SERVING: about 386 cal, 21 g pro, 24 g total fat (3 g sat. fat), 32 g carb, 7 g fibre, 0 mg chol, 844 mg sodium. % RDI: 30% calcium, 36% iron, 177% vit A, 58% vit C, 63% folate.

Brown Rice & Toasted Bean Salad

Toasted corn and beans have an earthy flavour – perfect when paired with brown rice, cheese and herbs in this exotic South American–style salad.

1 cup **brown rice**

1 cup **frozen corn kernels,** thawed

3 large **plum tomatoes,** halved lengthwise

6 **green onions**

1 can (19 oz/540 mL) **black beans,** drained and rinsed

¾ tsp each **dried oregano** and **ground cumin**

3 cups **baby arugula**

⅔ cup **hulled roasted pumpkin seeds** or sliced almonds

⅔ cup crumbled **feta cheese**

½ cup chopped **fresh cilantro**

DRESSING:

⅓ cup **extra-virgin olive oil**

3 tbsp **lime juice**

1 clove **garlic,** minced

½ tsp each **salt** and **pepper**

DRESSING: Whisk together oil, lime juice, garlic, salt and pepper; set aside.

In saucepan, bring rice and 2 cups water to boil; reduce heat, cover and simmer until no liquid remains, 30 to 35 minutes. Let cool for 10 minutes; fluff with fork.

Meanwhile, in cast-iron or other heavy skillet, toast corn over high heat, shaking pan, until fragrant and lightly charred, 1 to 2 minutes. Transfer to large bowl.

In same skillet, cook tomatoes and green onions, turning once, until softened and lightly charred, about 3 minutes. Let cool on cutting board; cut into small chunks and add to bowl.

Add black beans, oregano and cumin to skillet; cook until beans are dry and fragrant, about 2 minutes. Add to bowl. Stir in rice, arugula and pumpkin seeds.

Add dressing, feta cheese and cilantro; toss to coat.

Makes 4 servings. PER SERVING: about 758 cal, 30 g pro, 42 g total fat (10 g sat. fat), 74 g carb, 18 g fibre, 23 mg chol, 959 mg sodium, 1,154 mg potassium. % RDI: 26% calcium, 73% iron, 23% vit A, 37% vit C, 75% folate.

Watercress Soufflé

Bright green flecks of peppery watercress dot this dish. It's pretty and light-tasting – ideal as a luncheon or special dinner.

3 tbsp **butter**

2 tbsp finely grated **Parmesan cheese**

3 tbsp **all-purpose flour**

½ tsp **salt**

¼ tsp **pepper**

1 cup **milk**

8 **eggs,** separated

2 cups **watercress leaves,** finely chopped

½ tsp **Dijon mustard**

Grease 8- x 3¾-inch (2.5 L) soufflé dish with 1 tsp of the butter; sprinkle evenly with Parmesan cheese. Set aside.

In saucepan, melt remaining butter over medium heat. Stir in flour, salt and pepper; cook, stirring, for 1 minute. Whisk in milk; cook, whisking, until thickened, about 5 minutes. Pour into large bowl; whisk in egg yolks, watercress and mustard. Set aside.

In separate bowl, beat egg whites until stiff peaks form. Fold one-third into egg yolk mixture; fold in remaining whites. Pour into prepared dish.

Bake in 400°F (200°C) oven until puffed, dark golden and firm to the touch, about 30 minutes. Serve immediately.

Makes 4 to 6 servings. PER EACH OF 6 SERVINGS: about 193 cal, 11 g pro, 14 g total fat (7 g sat. fat), 6 g carb, trace fibre, 268 mg chol, 371 mg sodium. % RDI: 11% calcium, 7% iron, 21% vit A, 7% vit C, 20% folate.

Sugar Shack Crêpes With Ham & Eggs

Sometimes breakfast for dinner is the best option. The chives tend to sink to the bottom of the crêpes, so roll them chive side out for a pretty presentation.

8 slices **Black Forest ham**

6 **eggs**

Pinch each **salt** and **pepper**

1 tbsp **butter**

⅓ cup **maple syrup**

CHIVE CRÊPES:

⅔ cup **all-purpose flour**

Pinch **salt**

2 **eggs**

¾ cup **milk**

2 tbsp **butter,** melted and cooled

1 tbsp chopped **fresh chives**

CHIVE CRÊPES: In bowl, whisk flour with salt. Whisk together eggs, milk and half of the butter; pour over dry ingredients and whisk until smooth. Strain through fine sieve into bowl; stir in chives. Refrigerate for 1 hour or up to 2 hours.

Heat 8-inch (20 cm) crêpe pan or nonstick skillet over medium heat; brush with some of the remaining butter. Pour scant ¼ cup batter into centre of pan; using small offset spatula, spread batter to make thin circle. Cook, turning once, until golden, about 1 minute. Transfer to plate; keep warm. Repeat with remaining butter and batter to make 8 crêpes.

In same pan over medium heat, cook ham, in batches and turning once, until lightly browned and heated through, about 1 minute. Transfer to plate; keep warm. Wipe out pan.

Beat together 2 tbsp water, eggs, salt and pepper. In same pan, melt butter over medium heat; cook egg mixture, stirring gently with spatula, until large moist curds form and no liquid remains, about 3 minutes.

Top each crêpe with 1 slice ham and one-eighth of the scrambled eggs. Roll up. Arrange 2 crêpes on each of 4 plates; drizzle with maple syrup.

Makes 4 servings. PER SERVING: about 446 cal, 26 g pro, 21 g total fat (9 g sat. fat), 36 g carb, 1 g fibre, 428 mg chol, 917 mg sodium, 458 mg potassium. % RDI: 9% calcium, 21% iron, 23% vit A, 43% folate.

CANADIAN
CLASSIC

Spinach & Potato Baked Omelette

Omelettes are one of the most economical dinners you can make. This baked one puffs up to golden perfection in the oven rather than on the stove top.

1 large **potato,** peeled and halved (about 8 oz/225 g)

8 **eggs,** beaten

1 tbsp **all-purpose flour**

1 tsp **baking powder**

½ tsp **salt**

2 tbsp **extra-virgin olive oil**

1 large clove **garlic,** minced

Half bunch **spinach,** trimmed

Half **onion,** thinly sliced

¼ tsp **smoked paprika** or sweet paprika

In saucepan of boiling salted water, cook potato until tender, about 10 minutes. Drain and let cool. Cut into 1-inch (2.5 cm) chunks.

Meanwhile, whisk together eggs, flour, baking powder and half of the salt; set aside.

Meanwhile, in 9-inch (23 cm) ovenproof nonstick skillet, heat half of the oil over medium-high heat; sauté garlic for 1 minute. Add spinach; cook, stirring, until wilted and no liquid remains. Transfer to bowl.

Add remaining oil to skillet; cook onion, stirring occasionally, until softened, about 6 minutes. Add potato; cook, stirring, until softened and starting to brown. Stir in paprika and remaining salt. Stir in spinach, then egg mixture.

Transfer skillet to 350°F (180°C) oven; bake until firm, about 20 minutes.

Makes 4 to 6 servings. PER EACH OF 6 SERVINGS: about 195 cal, 10 g pro, 11 g total fat (3 g sat. fat), 14 g carb, 2 g fibre, 248 mg chol, 460 mg sodium, 382 mg potassium. % RDI: 9% calcium, 14% iron, 36% vit A, 10% vit C, 35% folate.

Mushroom & Goat Cheese Soufflé

No soufflé dish? Use an 8-inch (2 L) square baking dish instead; five minutes before the suggested cooking time, test the soufflé with a skewer. It should be moist but cooked through.

¼ cup **butter**

⅓ cup finely grated **Parmesan cheese**

1 large **shallot,** finely chopped

8 oz (225 g) **cremini mushrooms,** finely chopped

2 tsp finely chopped **fresh tarragon** (or ½ tsp dried)

¼ cup **all-purpose flour**

¼ tsp each **salt** and **pepper**

1¼ cups **milk**

6 **eggs,** separated

4 oz (115 g) **goat cheese**

Pinch **cream of tartar**

Grease 7- x 3-inch (1.5 L) soufflé dish with 2 tsp of the butter; sprinkle evenly with 3 tbsp of the Parmesan cheese. Set aside.

In skillet, melt 1 tbsp of the remaining butter over medium heat; cook shallot until translucent, about 3 minutes.

Stir in mushrooms and tarragon; cook, stirring, over medium-high heat until no liquid remains, about 5 minutes. Let cool.

In saucepan, melt remaining butter over medium heat; whisk in flour, salt and pepper. Cook, whisking, for 2 minutes. Gradually whisk in milk; cook, whisking, until thickened, about 4 minutes. Remove from heat.

Stir in egg yolks, goat cheese and remaining Parmesan cheese. Transfer to large bowl; let cool for 10 minutes. Fold in mushroom mixture.

In separate bowl, beat egg whites with cream of tartar until stiff peaks form. Fold one-third into mushroom mixture; fold in remaining whites. Scrape into prepared dish.

Bake on baking sheet in bottom third of 400°F (200°C) oven until puffed and golden, about 40 minutes. Serve immediately.

Makes 4 servings. PER SERVING: about 404 cal, 23 g pro, 29 g total fat (16 g sat. fat), 14 g carb, 2 g fibre, 336 mg chol, 583 mg sodium, 504 mg potassium. % RDI: 25% calcium, 16% iron, 34% vit A, 30% folate.

Budget-Friendly Eggs

What Makes Them Affordable: Eggs have been a cornerstone of affordable diets since people first domesticated chickens. And with the recent rediscovery of backyard chicken keeping – not to mention the growing interest in small-scale local producers – eggs are easy to find everywhere at reasonable prices.

Eggshells are designed to protect the contents within, so they are surprisingly adept at keeping out bacteria. While eggs are still considered perishable, they last quite a while, making them a low-waste staple that's always good to keep on hand.

Why They're Good for You: A large egg contains only 70 calories, but it's packed with nutrients. It's rich in easily digestible protein and supplies a number of vitamins and minerals, including iron; vitamins A, B_{12}, D and E; folate; selenium; and choline (a potent brain builder). The lutein and zeaxanthin in eggs help prevent cataracts and macular degeneration, two eye disorders that are common later in life.

Food Safety: To keep eggs fresh, the shells need to be free of cracks so that harmful bacteria don't get inside. Keep eggs in their carton, and don't store them in the fridge door, which is warmer than the interior. Keeping eggs in the carton also keeps away strong smells, which can be absorbed through the porous shells. Check the side of the carton for the best-by date and use up the eggs before then.

Uses: Eggs are simply delicious on their own: fried, boiled, scrambled, poached or stirred up into omelettes. They're vital to the texture of many baked goods, and the key to silky sauces, such as mayonnaise, and custards. Try whipping eggs into a soufflé (it's not as hard as it looks!) for a special dinner with friends. Or scramble them and add to stir-fries as a delicious vegetarian source of protein.

Eggs Florentine

Scrambled eggs combined with sautéed spinach are perfect any time.

1 tbsp **butter**

2 cloves **garlic,** minced

6 oz (170 g) **fresh baby spinach**

8 **eggs**

Pinch each **salt** and **pepper**

1 large **tomato,** seeded and diced

2 oz (55 g) **feta cheese,** crumbled

In large nonstick skillet, melt 1 tsp of the butter over medium-high heat; cook garlic until fragrant, about 30 seconds. Add spinach; cook, tossing, until wilted and any liquid is evaporated, about 5 minutes. Transfer to plate.

Meanwhile, in bowl, lightly beat together eggs, salt and pepper.

Melt remaining butter in skillet over medium heat; add eggs and cook, stirring with spatula, until almost set, about 3 minutes. Stir in spinach mixture until combined and eggs are just set.

Serve sprinkled with tomato and feta cheese.

make it a meal!

Breakfast for Dinner

Serve this simple scramble with toasted sliced baguette or whole wheat bread and fresh fruit for a complete, light meal.

Makes 4 servings. PER SERVING: about 228 cal, 16 g pro, 16 g total fat (7 g sat. fat), 5 g carb, 2 g fibre, 393 mg chol, 331 mg sodium, 438 mg potassium. % RDI: 17% calcium, 20% iron, 65% vit A, 17% vit C, 55% folate.

Roasted Tofu With Pepper Sauce

This meat-free dish is chewy and satisfying, and the delicious sauce requires only a few pantry-friendly ingredients – and a few minutes – to make.

1 pkg (1 lb/454 g) **extra-firm tofu,** drained

1 jar (370 mL) **roasted red peppers**

2 tbsp **extra-virgin olive oil**

2 cloves **garlic,** minced

1 tsp **sweet paprika**

¼ tsp each **salt** and **pepper**

1 tbsp **vegetable oil**

Pat tofu dry; cut crosswise into eight ½-inch (1 cm) thick slices. Set aside.

Drain, rinse and pat red peppers dry. In blender, purée together peppers, olive oil, 2 tbsp water, garlic, paprika, salt and pepper. Pour marinade into shallow glass baking dish; add tofu, turning to coat. Let stand for 10 minutes. *(Make-ahead: Cover and refrigerate for up to 24 hours.)*

In skillet, heat vegetable oil over medium-high heat. Scraping any marinade clinging to tofu back into baking dish, add tofu, in batches, to skillet. Fry, adding more vegetable oil if necessary and turning once, until browned, about 6 minutes.

Return fried tofu to reserved marinade. Roast in 350°F (180°C) oven for 15 minutes.

how to

Give Tofu a Meaty Texture

This recipe is even better made with tofu that has been frozen. Freezing tofu gives it a denser, meatier texture, and the longer it stays frozen, the denser it becomes. To freeze, cut into at least ¼-inch (5 mm) thick slices; freeze in single layer in airtight container for up to 1 month. Thaw in refrigerator to use.

Makes 4 servings. PER SERVING: about 218 cal, 13 g pro, 17 g total fat (2 g sat. fat), 7 g carb, 2 g fibre, 0 mg chol, 285 mg sodium. % RDI: 16% calcium, 17% iron, 23% vit A, 158% vit C, 18% folate.

Black Bean & Scrambled Egg Enchiladas

Eggs and beans are both great sources of protein. Here, they make a substantial filling in a popular Mexican main dish.

1 can (19 oz/540 mL) **black beans,** drained and rinsed

1 can (4½ oz/127 mL) **chopped green chilies,** drained

1 tbsp **lime juice**

12 **eggs**

3 **green onions,** thinly sliced

¼ tsp each **salt** and **pepper**

2 tbsp **butter**

8 large **tortillas**

¾ cup shredded **Monterey Jack cheese**

ENCHILADA SAUCE:

1 tbsp **olive oil**

1 **red onion,** diced

1 clove **garlic,** minced

1 bottle (680 mL) **strained tomatoes** (passata)

1 cup **vegetable broth**

2 tsp **chili powder**

1 tsp **dried oregano**

¼ tsp **salt**

¼ cup chopped **fresh cilantro**

ENCHILADA SAUCE: In saucepan, heat oil over medium heat; fry onion and garlic until onion is softened, about 3 minutes. Stir in tomatoes, broth, chili powder, oregano and salt; bring to boil. Reduce heat and simmer for 15 minutes. Stir in cilantro.

In bowl, combine beans, green chilies, lime juice and ½ cup of the enchilada sauce; mash with fork. Set aside.

Beat together eggs, ¼ cup water, half of the green onions, the salt and pepper.

In skillet, melt butter over medium heat; cook eggs, stirring, just until softly set but still moist.

Divide bean mixture among tortillas, spreading evenly. Spoon egg mixture along bottom third of each; roll up tortilla. Trim ends; place, seam side down, in greased 13- x 9-inch (3 L) baking dish. Spoon 3 cups of the remaining sauce over top. Sprinkle with cheese and remaining green onions.

Bake in 375°F (190°C) oven until hot and bubbly, about 30 minutes. Serve with remaining sauce.

Makes 8 servings. PER SERVING: about 517 cal, 22 g pro, 21 g total fat (8 g sat. fat), 59 g carb, 7 g fibre, 297 mg chol, 1,138 mg sodium, 439 mg potassium. % RDI: 17% calcium, 44% iron, 19% vit A, 12% vit C, 77% folate.

MAKE IT
THE NIGHT
BEFORE

Spinach, Ham & Cheese Strata

Strata is a savoury type of bread pudding that's delicious for dinner or brunch. If you have any leftover sourdough bread, it makes wonderful toast or croutons.

1 tbsp **olive oil**

1 bunch (10 oz/280 g) **spinach,** chopped

1 clove **garlic,** minced

¼ tsp each **salt** and **pepper**

6 cups cubed (1 inch/2.5 cm) **sourdough bread**

3 **green onions,** thinly sliced

¾ cup shredded **Swiss cheese**

½ cup chopped **sliced ham**

4 **eggs**

1¼ cups **milk**

1½ tsp **Dijon mustard**

In skillet, heat oil over medium-high heat; sauté spinach, garlic, salt and pepper until spinach is wilted and no liquid remains.

Stir together spinach mixture, bread, green onions, cheese and ham. Spread in greased 8-inch (2 L) square baking dish.

Whisk together eggs, milk and mustard; pour over bread mixture and let stand for 20 minutes. *(Make-ahead: Cover and refrigerate for up to 24 hours.)*

Bake in 375°F (190°C) oven until puffed and golden, about 45 minutes.

Makes 4 servings. PER SERVING: about 411 cal, 26 g pro, 18 g total fat (7 g sat. fat), 36 g carb, 4 g fibre, 220 mg chol, 899 mg sodium, 661 mg potassium. % RDI: 38% calcium, 34% iron, 87% vit A, 13% vit C, 78% folate.

Pineapple Tofu With Cashews

Stir-fries are terrific last-minute dinners. This one has the sweetness of pineapple and the crunch of cashews to complement nutrient-rich tofu.

1 pkg (1 lb/454 g) **firm tofu** or extra-firm tofu, drained

2 tbsp **vegetable oil**

2 **green onions,** sliced

1 clove **garlic,** minced

1 **sweet red pepper,** diced

2 tbsp **sodium-reduced soy sauce**

1 tsp grated **fresh ginger**

¼ tsp **salt**

Pinch **hot pepper flakes**

1 can (14 oz/398 mL) **pineapple tidbits**

½ cup **unsalted roasted cashews**

1 tsp **cornstarch**

2 tbsp chopped **fresh cilantro**

Pat tofu dry; cut into 1-inch (2.5 cm) cubes. In large skillet, heat oil over medium-high heat; fry tofu until golden and crisp on edges, about 7 minutes.

Add green onions, garlic, red pepper, soy sauce, ginger, salt and hot pepper flakes; fry over medium heat, gently stirring occasionally, until softened, about 3 minutes.

Stir in pineapple with juice and cashews; bring to boil. Reduce heat and simmer until almost no liquid remains, about 5 minutes.

Whisk cornstarch with 1 tbsp water; stir into tofu mixture and simmer until clear and glossy, about 1 minute. Stir in cilantro.

Makes 4 servings. PER SERVING: about 323 cal, 13 g pro, 20 g total fat (3 g sat. fat), 29 g carb, 4 g fibre, 0 mg chol, 459 mg sodium. % RDI: 20% calcium, 22% iron, 12% vit A, 95% vit C, 27% folate.

Chicken & Egg Donburi

Served over steaming rice, this traditional Japanese egg-and-chicken dish is the ultimate comforting weeknight dinner.

3 **eggs**

Pinch **pepper**

2 tbsp **mirin**

4 tsp **soy sauce**

2 tsp **granulated sugar**

¾ cup thinly sliced **sweet onion**

4 **boneless skinless chicken thighs,** cut in 1-inch (2.5 cm) chunks

2 **green onions,** cut in chunks

2 cups lightly packed **watercress leaves and stems** (optional)

1 cup sliced **cremini mushrooms**

1½ cups **hot cooked rice**

In bowl, beat eggs with pepper; set aside.

In glass measure, whisk together ½ cup water, mirin, soy sauce and sugar; set aside.

Sprinkle sweet onion evenly in nonstick skillet; top with chicken, green onions, watercress (if using) and mushrooms. Pour soy sauce mixture over top; cover and simmer over medium heat until juices run clear when chicken is pierced, 3 to 5 minutes.

Pour eggs over chicken mixture; cover and simmer over low heat until lightly set, about 30 seconds. Serve over rice.

don't waste it!

Leftover Rice

This recipe is great when you have just a little cooked rice left after the previous night's dinner.

Makes 2 or 3 servings. PER EACH OF 3 SERVINGS: about 341 cal, 25 g pro, 9 g total fat (3 g sat. fat), 37 g carb, 2 g fibre, 250 mg chol, 534 mg sodium, 464 mg potassium. % RDI: 6% calcium, 14% iron, 9% vit A, 7% vit C, 21% folate.

Gardener's Pie

Vegetarians should be able to enjoy shepherd's pie, too. This recipe is made with ready-to-eat soy protein, which has a surprisingly meaty taste and texture.

1 tbsp **vegetable oil**

1 **onion,** chopped

1 **carrot,** diced

1 tsp **dried basil**

¼ tsp **pepper**

1 pkg (340 g) **precooked ground soy protein mixture** (such as Yves Veggie Ground Round)

1 can (19 oz/540 mL) **black beans,** drained and rinsed

2 tbsp **all-purpose flour**

1 cup **vegetable broth**

2 tbsp **tomato paste**

POTATO TOPPING:

3 **potatoes** (1½ lb/675 g)

¼ cup **milk**

Pinch each **salt** and **pepper**

In large skillet, heat oil over medium-high heat; cook onion, carrot, basil and pepper, stirring occasionally, until golden, about 10 minutes.

Add ground soy and beans. Sprinkle with flour; cook, stirring, for 1 minute. Add broth and tomato paste; bring to boil and boil, stirring, for 2 minutes. Scrape into greased 8-inch (2 L) square baking dish.

POTATO TOPPING: Meanwhile, peel potatoes and cut into chunks. In saucepan of boiling salted water, cook potatoes until tender, 12 to 15 minutes. Drain and return to pot; mash with milk, salt and pepper. Spread over vegetable mixture.

Bake in 400°F (200°C) oven until hot, about 20 minutes. Broil until golden.

Makes 4 servings. PER SERVING: about 388 cal, 26 g pro, 4 g total fat (1 g sat. fat), 62 g carb, 15 g fibre, 2 mg chol, 1,317 mg sodium. % RDI: 13% calcium, 50% iron, 35% vit A, 25% vit C, 39% folate.

CLASSIC
WITH
A TWIST

Crispy Tofu With Two Sauces

This recipe makes more ginger-flavoured oil than you need. Use the leftovers to stir-fry sliced red peppers and snow peas for a colourful, tasty side dish.

1 pkg (1 lb/454 g) **medium-firm tofu,** drained

½ cup **peanut oil**

½ cup **cornstarch**

GREEN ONION GINGER SAUCE:

3 **green onions,** finely chopped

2 tbsp grated **fresh ginger**

1 tsp **kosher salt**

¼ cup **peanut oil**

SPICY SOY SAUCE:

2 tbsp **soy sauce**

1 tsp **seasoned rice vinegar**

¼ tsp grated **fresh ginger**

¼ tsp **sriracha** or chili paste

¼ tsp **liquid honey**

Cut tofu into 4 equal slices, about 1 inch (2.5 cm) thick. Place, cut side down, on triple-thickness paper towel to drain; let stand for 20 minutes. Pat dry.

GREEN ONION GINGER SAUCE: Meanwhile, in 2-cup heatproof glass measure, combine green onions, ginger and salt. In small saucepan, heat oil over medium-high heat just until ripples form on surface; pour over onion mixture until sizzling. Stir to combine. Let cool for 5 minutes. Drain off 2 tbsp of the oil and reserve for another use. Set sauce aside.

SPICY SOY SAUCE: Stir together soy sauce, 1 tbsp water, vinegar, ginger, sriracha and honey. Set aside.

In 10-inch (25 cm) skillet, heat oil over medium heat. Coat tofu all over with cornstarch; fry, turning once, until golden and crispy, 8 to 10 minutes. Serve with sauces.

Makes 4 servings. PER SERVING: about 440 cal, 17 g pro, 33 g total fat (5 g sat. fat), 20 g carb, 1 g fibre, 0 mg chol, 823 mg sodium, 230 mg potassium. % RDI: 17% calcium, 16% iron, 1% vit A, 2% vit C, 12% folate.

Eggplant & Tofu in Spicy Meat Sauce

If you crave even more heat, use chili oil instead of the sesame oil in this dish. Stand back when you add the chili flakes – the chili oil can sting your eyes.

1 **eggplant** (about 12 oz/340 g), unpeeled

1 tsp **salt**

Half pkg (1 lb/454 g pkg) **firm tofu,** drained

2 tbsp **vegetable oil**

½ tsp **hot pepper flakes**

8 oz (225 g) **lean ground beef**

3 cloves **garlic,** minced

1 tsp minced **fresh ginger**

¼ tsp **pepper**

2 tbsp **dry sherry** (optional)

2 tbsp **soy sauce**

½ tsp **granulated sugar**

1 cup **sodium-reduced chicken broth**

2 tsp **cornstarch**

2 **green onions,** chopped

1 tsp **sesame oil**

Cut eggplant into ½-inch (1 cm) cubes. In bowl, toss eggplant with salt; let stand for 15 minutes. Rinse thoroughly under cold running water; drain in colander, pressing lightly.

Meanwhile, cut tofu into ½-inch (1 cm) cubes; set aside.

In wok or large skillet, heat vegetable oil over high heat; add hot pepper flakes. Add beef, garlic, ginger and pepper; stir-fry until beef is lightly browned, about 4 minutes. Add sherry (if using); cook for 1 minute. Add soy sauce and sugar; cook for 1 minute.

Add eggplant; stir-fry for 2 minutes. Add tofu and broth; cook, stirring gently to keep tofu in cubes, until eggplant is tender, about 3 minutes.

Mix cornstarch with 1 tbsp water; stir into sauce. Add green onions; cook for 1 minute. Stir in sesame oil.

Makes 4 servings. PER SERVING: about 284 cal, 19 g pro, 19 g total fat (4 g sat. fat), 13 g carb, 3 g fibre, 34 mg chol, 870 mg sodium, 410 mg potassium. % RDI: 14% calcium, 19% iron, 2% vit A, 5% vit C, 15% folate.

READY IN
20 MINUTES

Broiled Tofu With No-Cook Peanut Sauce

Broiling tofu makes it crispy without the hassle of deep-frying. The versatile peanut sauce can double as a veggie dip or a sauce for cold pasta or chicken.

1 pkg (1 lb/454 g) **firm tofu,** drained and cut in 8 slices

2 tbsp **olive oil**

1 large stalk **broccoli,** stems removed and separated into florets

1 tbsp toasted **sesame seeds**

NO-COOK PEANUT SAUCE:

¼ cup **reduced-fat peanut butter**

1 tbsp grated **fresh ginger**

2 tsp each **sodium-reduced soy sauce** and **unseasoned rice vinegar**

1 tsp **sesame oil**

½ tsp **Asian chili paste** (such as sambal oelek)

2 **green onions,** thinly sliced

Between paper towels, pat tofu dry. Brush baking sheet with 1 tsp of the oil. Arrange tofu on pan; brush remaining oil over top. Broil, about 8 inches (20 cm) from heat, until crisp and dry looking, about 15 minutes.

Meanwhile, in steamer, cover and steam broccoli until tender-crisp, about 3 minutes.

NO-COOK PEANUT SAUCE: Meanwhile, in small bowl, whisk together peanut butter, ginger, soy sauce, vinegar, sesame oil and chili paste; slowly whisk in ¼ cup hot water. Stir in green onions.

Serve tofu over broccoli. Drizzle with peanut sauce; sprinkle with sesame seeds.

Makes 4 servings. PER SERVING: about 347 cal, 22 g pro, 24 g total fat (3 g sat. fat), 15 g carb, 4 g fibre, 0 mg chol, 241 mg sodium, 461 mg potassium. % RDI: 21% calcium, 23% iron, 22% vit A, 73% vit C, 38% folate.

chapter four

Cheesy Baked
Sausage-Stuffed
Shells, page 178

Pasta, Noodles & Rice

Vegetable Pho

This is a meatless version of the very popular Vietnamese pho, a hearty beef-based noodle soup. Serve with garnishes such as cilantro, sliced green onions, sliced hot peppers, bean sprouts and lime wedges.

2 tsp **vegetable oil**

Half **onion,** thinly sliced

¾ tsp **five-spice powder**

1 cup thinly sliced **shiitake mushroom caps**

2 tsp grated **fresh ginger**

¼ tsp **salt**

1 pkg (900 mL) **sodium-reduced vegetable broth**

1 **carrot,** julienned

8 oz (225 g) **baby bok choy,** quartered

2 tsp **lime juice**

12 oz (340 g) **rice stick vermicelli** (about ⅓ inch/8 mm)

Half pkg (350 g pkg) **extra-firm tofu,** thinly sliced

Pinch **hot pepper flakes** (optional)

In saucepan, heat oil over medium-high heat; cook onion and five-spice powder, stirring occasionally, until onion is softened, about 3 minutes. Add mushrooms, ginger and salt; cook for 2 minutes.

Add broth and 1½ cups water; bring to boil. Reduce heat and simmer for 5 minutes.

Add carrot, bok choy and lime juice; cook until bok choy is slightly softened, about 1 minute.

Meanwhile, in pot of boiling water, cook noodles according to package directions. Drain and rinse under cold water. Divide among 4 large soup bowls. Top with tofu. Ladle hot broth and vegetables over top. Sprinkle with hot pepper flakes (if using).

Makes 4 servings. PER SERVING: about 432 cal, 11 g pro, 7 g total fat (1 g sat. fat), 81 g carb, 6 g fibre, 0 mg chol, 374 mg sodium, 433 mg potassium. % RDI: 16% calcium, 19% iron, 58% vit A, 28% vit C, 22% folate.

EASY
VEGAN

Chicken Pilaf With Spinach & Walnuts

Toasted walnuts and fresh herbs bring a pleasant crunch and bright flavour to this Mediterranean-inspired dish.

½ cup chopped **walnuts**

1 lb (450 g) **boneless skinless chicken thighs,** cubed

¾ tsp **salt**

½ tsp **pepper**

2 tbsp **olive oil**

1 **onion,** diced

1 clove **garlic,** minced

1 cup **basmati rice** or other long-grain white rice

½ tsp **ground cumin**

¼ tsp **ground allspice**

Pinch **cinnamon**

4 cups loosely packed **fresh baby spinach,** coarsely chopped

2 tbsp chopped **fresh dill**

On rimmed baking sheet, toast walnuts in 350°F (180°C) oven until golden, about 8 minutes. Set aside.

Sprinkle chicken with half each of the salt and pepper. In large saucepan, heat oil over medium-high heat; brown chicken. Using slotted spoon, transfer to bowl.

In same saucepan, cook onion and garlic over medium heat until slightly softened, about 2 minutes. Stir in rice, cumin, allspice, cinnamon and remaining salt and pepper; cook, stirring, for 2 minutes. Return chicken and any accumulated juices to pan, stirring to coat.

Stir in 1¾ cups water; bring to boil. Reduce heat, cover and simmer until rice is tender and no liquid remains, about 20 minutes. Turn off heat; let stand on burner for 5 minutes.

Stir in spinach, dill and toasted walnuts.

know your ingredients
The Freshest Walnuts

California walnut halves are the best choice for flavour and freshness. Chopped nuts and pieces can go rancid quickly, so it's best to chop halves yourself.

Makes 4 servings. PER SERVING: about 489 cal, 29 g pro, 23 g total fat (3 g sat. fat), 43 g carb, 3 g fibre, 94 mg chol, 553 mg sodium, 560 mg potassium. % RDI: 8% calcium, 24% iron, 32% vit A, 10% vit C, 33% folate.

Salmon Kedgeree

A traditional British breakfast dish, this mix of fish and curry-scented rice makes a tasty, simple dinner. Fish can be expensive, but this recipe stretches a little a long way. It's also great with trout – a plus if you know someone who likes to fish.

8 oz (225 g) **skinless salmon fillet**

1 tsp **vegetable oil**

¾ tsp **salt**

¼ tsp **pepper**

1 tbsp **ghee** (clarified butter) or vegetable oil

1 small **onion,** chopped

2 tsp minced **fresh ginger**

2 tsp **curry powder**

¼ tsp **turmeric**

3 **green cardamom pods,** smashed (optional)

1 **bay leaf**

1 cup **basmati rice**

1½ cups **sodium-reduced chicken broth**

1 cup **frozen peas**

2 tbsp chopped **fresh cilantro** or parsley

4 to 6 **hard-cooked eggs** (see How-To, page 237), quartered

On greased baking sheet, brush salmon with oil; sprinkle with half each of the salt and pepper. Bake in 400°F (200°C) oven until fish flakes easily when tested, about 20 minutes. Flake into about 2-inch (5 cm) chunks; set aside.

Meanwhile, in saucepan, heat ghee over medium heat; cook onion until softened and golden, about 8 minutes.

Stir in ginger, curry powder, turmeric, cardamom pods (if using), bay leaf, and remaining salt and pepper; cook until fragrant, about 30 seconds. Stir in rice; cook, stirring, for 1 minute.

Add broth and bring to boil; reduce heat, cover and simmer until rice is tender and no liquid remains, about 20 minutes. Remove from heat. Stir in peas and cilantro; let stand, covered, for 2 minutes. Discard bay leaf.

Gently stir in salmon. Transfer to platter; arrange eggs on top.

Makes 4 servings. PER SERVING: about 413 cal, 23 g pro, 15 g total fat (5 g sat. fat), 45 g carb, 3 g fibre, 222 mg chol, 765 mg sodium, 369 mg potassium. % RDI: 6% calcium, 14% iron, 18% vit A, 8% vit C, 30% folate.

Japanese Cold Noodle "Chef Salad"

Sliced mushrooms, tofu, and shredded cabbage or carrots are also nice in this summery dinner. Toast sesame seeds briefly in a dry skillet.

2 **eggs**

Pinch **salt**

1 tbsp **vegetable oil**

12 oz (340 g) **Chinese wheat noodles** or ramen

2 tsp **sesame oil**

8 oz (225 g) sliced **deli ham,** julienned

1 **sweet red pepper,** very thinly sliced

1 cup shredded **English cucumber**

4 cups shredded **iceberg lettuce**

2 **green onions,** thinly sliced

4 tsp toasted **sesame seeds**

SAUCE:

⅔ cup **chicken broth**

⅓ cup **granulated sugar**

⅓ cup **unseasoned rice vinegar** or cider vinegar

3 tbsp **soy sauce**

1 tbsp grated **fresh ginger**

SAUCE: In saucepan, bring broth, sugar, vinegar, soy sauce and ginger to boil; reduce heat and simmer for 5 minutes. Strain and refrigerate until cool. (Make-ahead: Refrigerate in airtight container for up to 3 days.)

Beat together eggs, salt and 1 tsp of the vegetable oil. Heat 6-inch (15 cm) nonstick skillet over medium-high heat; brush lightly with some of the remaining vegetable oil. Pour in about one-quarter of the egg mixture, tilting pan to spread evenly; cook until top is set, about 30 seconds. Slide out onto cutting board. Repeat with remaining egg mixture to make 4 thin omelettes; stack and cut into fine shreds.

In large pot of boiling salted water, cook noodles until tender but firm, about 5 minutes. Drain and chill under cold water; drain well. In bowl, toss noodles with sesame oil.

Arrange noodles on 4 plates. Attractively top with eggs, ham, red pepper, cucumber and lettuce. Sprinkle with green onions. (Make-ahead: Cover and refrigerate for up to 4 hours.)

Sprinkle with sauce and sesame seeds.

Makes 4 servings. PER SERVING: about 696 cal, 27 g pro, 30 g total fat (10 g sat. fat), 81 g carb, 6 g fibre, 120 mg chol, 1,986 mg sodium. % RDI: 7% calcium, 22% iron, 24% vit A, 103% vit C, 37% folate.

Homemade Fettuccine

Pasta making requires an initial investment in equipment, but it's a good money saver after that. Homemade pasta tastes so much better than dried that you'll never want to go back – and it only takes two minutes to boil to al dente perfection.

2 cups **all-purpose flour**

3 **eggs**

¼ tsp **salt**

Mound flour on work surface; make well in centre. Break eggs into well; sprinkle with salt. Using fork, beat eggs. Starting at inside edge and working around well, gradually incorporate flour into egg mixture until soft dough forms. Scoop up and sift flour left on work surface, discarding any bits of dough; set aside.

On lightly floured surface, knead dough, dusting with sifted flour, until smooth and elastic, about 10 minutes. Cover with plastic wrap; let rest for 20 minutes. Cut into thirds.

Keeping remaining dough covered to prevent drying out, roll or press 1 piece into 5-inch (12 cm) wide strip; dust with flour. Set pasta machine rollers to widest setting; dust rollers with flour. Feed dough through rollers; fold dough in half and lightly dust with flour. Feed dough lengthwise through rollers 3 more times or until edges are smooth. Without folding but cutting dough in half if too long to handle easily, continue feeding dough through rollers until next-to-finest setting is reached. Lightly flour dough; run through finest setting. Repeat with remaining dough.

Hang pasta strips on pasta drying rack or over back of chair; let stand until leathery but not dry, 15 to 20 minutes. (If dough dries, remove from rack and pat with damp cloth.)

Feed dough through fettuccine slicing attachment of pasta machine.

change it up!

Herbed Fettuccine

Add ¼ cup finely chopped fresh herbs (such as parsley, chives, basil or tarragon) to egg mixture.

Makes 12 oz (340 g), enough for 4 servings. PER SERVING (COOKED): about 282 cal, 11 g pro, 4 g total fat (1 g sat. fat), 48 g carb, 2 g fibre, 140 mg chol, 190 mg sodium, 113 mg potassium. % RDI: 3% calcium, 24% iron, 5% vit A, 66% folate.

Marinara Sauce

Use this easy, versatile sauce on pizza or Homemade Fettuccine (opposite), or as a dip for warm breadsticks. Make a double or triple batch and freeze 1-cup portions in airtight containers to use instead of store-bought pasta sauce.

1 tbsp **olive oil**

1 **onion,** diced

1 clove **garlic,** chopped

1 can (28 oz/796 mL) **whole tomatoes**

1 tbsp **balsamic vinegar**

¼ tsp **granulated sugar**

¼ cup thinly sliced **fresh basil** (optional)

In saucepan, heat oil over medium heat; cook onion, stirring occasionally, until golden, about 3 minutes. Add garlic; cook until fragrant, about 1 minute.

Stir in tomatoes, vinegar and sugar, breaking up tomatoes with spoon. Bring to boil; reduce heat and simmer, stirring occasionally, until thickened, about 30 minutes. Purée until smooth. Stir in basil (if using). *(Make-ahead: Refrigerate in airtight container for up to 3 days or freeze for up to 1 month.)*

change it up!

Arrabbiata Sauce

For a little bit of heat, add ¼ tsp hot pepper flakes along with the garlic. If you like your sauce even spicier, increase the hot pepper flakes to ½ tsp.

Makes about 3 cups. PER ¼ CUP: about 27 cal, 1 g pro, 1 g total fat (trace sat. fat), 4 g carb, 1 g fibre, 0 mg chol, 86 mg sodium, 142 mg potassium. % RDI: 2% calcium, 5% iron, 1% vit A, 15% vit C, 2% folate.

Gemelli With Kale, Sage & Potatoes

Pasta with potatoes? Yes, please. This satisfying dish get its rich taste from earthy kale, meaty pancetta (unsmoked Italian bacon) and creamy Fontina cheese.

1 bunch **kale** (about 1 lb/450 g)

2 tbsp **extra-virgin olive oil**

2 **yellow-fleshed potatoes,** peeled and cut in 1-inch (2.5 cm) cubes

⅓ cup chopped **pancetta**

2 cloves **garlic,** minced

4 tsp chopped **fresh sage**

¼ tsp **salt**

¼ tsp **hot pepper flakes**

10 oz (280 g) **gemelli pasta** or fusilli pasta (2½ cups)

1 cup **sodium-reduced chicken broth**

½ cup cubed (¼ inch/5 mm) **Fontina cheese** or grated Parmesan cheese

2 tsp **lemon juice**

Trim tough stems and ribs off kale. Coarsely chop leaves to make 10 cups. In large pot of boiling salted water, cover and cook kale until tender, about 3 minutes. Drain and chill in cold water; drain again and squeeze dry. Set aside. (*Make-ahead: Refrigerate in airtight container for up to 24 hours.*)

In nonstick skillet, heat oil over medium-high heat; sauté potatoes until golden, about 15 minutes. Add pancetta, garlic, sage, salt and hot pepper flakes; sauté for 3 minutes.

Meanwhile, in large pot of boiling salted water, cook pasta until al dente, about 8 minutes. Drain and return to pot.

Stir in kale, potato mixture, broth, Fontina cheese and lemon juice; cook, tossing to coat, until heated through, about 3 minutes.

change it up!

Vegetarian Gemelli With Kale, Sage & Potatoes

Omit pancetta. Replace chicken broth with pasta cooking liquid or vegetable broth. Sprinkle with ¼ cup grated Parmesan cheese before serving.

Makes 6 servings. PER SERVING: about 412 cal, 14 g pro, 17 g total fat (7 g sat. fat), 52 g carb, 4 g fibre, 26 mg chol, 661 mg sodium. % RDI: 15% calcium, 21% iron, 71% vit A, 90% vit C, 52% folate.

Budget-Friendly Pasta & Noodles

What Makes Them Affordable: Pasta and noodles are uncomplicated to make – they're a simple mixture of flour, water and maybe an egg – so they're a mainstay of the frugal cook. Whole grain versions can be a little pricier, but overall they're still reasonable for such a versatile staple.

Dried pasta keeps very well, so you won't waste any, even if it sits for a long time in the cupboard. Fresh pasta – especially homemade – needs to be used up quickly, but it has a pleasing, chewy texture that's unparalleled.

Why They're Good for You: While they're sometimes villainized for their high carbohydrate content, many types of pasta and noodles are low in fat and sodium. White pasta is usually enriched with vitamins and minerals, such as folic acid and iron. But if you choose whole grain pasta, you'll be getting a healthy dose of fibre, antioxidants and other nutrients that aren't added back to enriched white pasta. Rice noodles are filling and virtually fat-free; they aren't calorie-free, though, so it's best not to go overboard eating them.

Food Safety: Dried pasta and noodles are shelf stable, which makes them a pantry must-have. One of the best ways to store them is in sealed glass jars on a cool, dry shelf. Fresh pasta needs to be eaten within a couple days of making (or opening, in the case of store-bought). Wrap them tightly before refrigerating to keep them from drying out.

Uses: Thanks to their storability and quick cooking times, pasta and noodles can be the key to affordable, last-minute feasts. Pasta goes with all kinds of sauces, from simple red ones based on canned tomatoes to fancier cream- or cheese-based sauces. Try whole grain pastas with heartier sauces that will complement their nutty, earthy flavours. Rice noodles just need a quick soak, then they're ready for serving in soups or for stir-frying with vegetables. Asian wheat noodles, such as soba, udon, ramen or Chinese wheat noodles, are also wonderful in soups, stir-fries and noodle salads.

Seared Cherry Tomato Pasta

This pasta has few ingredients, cooks up in a snap and is a wonderful way to use up an abundance of cherry tomatoes from the garden. It's perfect for a main dish but also makes a lovely first course for six to eight people.

12 oz (340 g) **spaghettini**

2 tbsp **olive oil**

2 cups **cherry tomatoes,** halved

2 tbsp **dry bread crumbs**

½ tsp **salt**

3 cloves **garlic,** sliced

Pinch **hot pepper flakes**

⅓ cup grated **Parmesan cheese**

¼ cup chopped **fresh basil**

In large pot of boiling lightly salted water, cook pasta until al dente. Reserving ½ cup of the cooking liquid, drain.

Meanwhile, in large skillet, heat 1 tbsp of the oil over medium-high heat; sauté tomatoes until lightly seared, about 1 minute. Sprinkle with bread crumbs and salt; toss to coat. Remove from pan; set aside.

Add remaining oil to pan; cook garlic and hot pepper flakes over medium heat until fragrant and softened, about 2 minutes. Add tomato mixture, pasta and reserved cooking liquid, stirring to combine. Toss with Parmesan cheese and basil.

Makes 4 servings. PER SERVING: about 442 cal, 15 g pro, 11 g total fat (3 g sat. fat), 70 g carb, 5 g fibre, 7 mg chol, 714 mg sodium, 284 mg potassium. % RDI: 12% calcium, 26% iron, 8% vit A, 17% vit C, 85% folate.

FRESHLY
PICKED

Linguine With Watercress Pesto

This elegantly simple dish looks (and tastes) like a million bucks. No one has to know how cheaply – and easily – it comes together. Garnish with a few more coarsely chopped walnuts if you like a little extra crunch.

1 lb (450 g) **linguine pasta**

½ cup toasted **walnut halves**

2 cloves **garlic,** chopped

4 cups loosely packed trimmed **watercress** (about 1 large bunch)

½ cup tightly packed **fresh parsley**

⅓ cup **extra-virgin olive oil**

½ tsp **salt**

In large pot of boiling salted water, cook pasta until al dente, 10 to 12 minutes. Reserving ½ cup of the cooking liquid, drain; return pasta to pot.

Meanwhile, in blender, pulse walnuts with garlic until coarsely chopped. Add watercress, parsley, oil and salt; purée until smooth, scraping down side. Stir into pasta along with ¼ cup of the reserved cooking liquid, adding more as needed until sauce coats pasta.

Makes 4 servings. PER SERVING: about 684 cal, 18 g pro, 30 g total fat (4 g sat. fat), 88 g carb, 7 g fibre, 0 mg chol, 628 mg sodium, 317 mg potassium. % RDI: 8% calcium, 38% iron, 20% vit A, 37% vit C, 116% folate.

Italian Stove-Top Mac & Cheese

You can prepare this dinner favourite in minutes with ingredients you probably already have in your pantry.

2 tbsp **butter**

Half **onion,** finely diced

2 cloves **garlic,** minced

¾ tsp **dried Italian herb seasoning**

3 tbsp **all-purpose flour**

2 cups **milk**

2 tsp **Dijon mustard**

¼ tsp **salt**

1 cup shredded **old Cheddar cheese**

1 **plum tomato,** diced

2 tsp **pesto**

2½ cups **elbow macaroni** (12 oz/340 g)

¼ cup grated **Parmesan cheese**

In large saucepan or Dutch oven, melt butter over medium heat; cook onion, garlic and Italian herb seasoning, stirring occasionally, until onion is softened, 3 to 4 minutes.

Sprinkle with flour; cook, stirring, for 2 minutes. Gradually whisk in milk, mustard and salt; cook, whisking, until thickened, 4 to 5 minutes. Stir in Cheddar cheese until smooth.

Meanwhile, combine tomato with pesto; set aside.

Meanwhile, in large pot of boiling salted water, cook pasta until al dente; drain and return to pot. Add sauce and toss to coat. Serve sprinkled with tomato mixture and Parmesan cheese.

Makes 4 servings. PER SERVING: about 612 cal, 25 g pro, 22 g total fat (13 g sat. fat), 77 g carb, 5 g fibre, 60 mg chol, 782 mg sodium, 369 mg potassium. % RDI: 41% calcium, 28% iron, 21% vit A, 3% vit C, 90% folate.

Creamy Ham & Pea Pasta

Here's a great way to use up leftover ham after a holiday meal. Throw in any other vegetables you may have instead of (or in addition to) the peas.

2 tbsp **unsalted butter**

1 small **onion,** thinly sliced

1 clove **garlic,** minced

2 tbsp **all-purpose flour**

1 cup **sodium-reduced chicken broth**

1 cup **evaporated milk**

1 tbsp **grainy mustard**

2 cups cubed **cooked ham**

1 cup **frozen peas**

12 oz (340 g) **farfalle pasta**

In large skillet, melt butter over medium heat; cook onion, stirring occasionally, until golden, about 7 minutes.

Add garlic; cook for 1 minute. Stir in flour; cook, stirring, until light golden, about 1 minute. Whisk in broth, evaporated milk and mustard; cook, stirring occasionally, until slightly thickened, about 3 minutes. Stir in ham and peas; cook until hot, about 2 minutes.

Meanwhile, in large pot of boiling salted water, cook pasta until al dente. Reserving ¼ cup of the cooking liquid, drain; return pasta to pot. Add ham mixture and toss to coat, gradually thinning with reserved cooking liquid until sauce coats pasta.

Makes 4 servings. PER SERVING: about 593 cal, 34 g pro, 14 g total fat (7 g sat. fat), 80 g carb, 6 g fibre, 60 mg chol, 1,486 mg sodium, 596 mg potassium. % RDI: 20% calcium, 36% iron, 16% vit A, 43% vit C, 94% folate.

Bruschetta Penne

A handful of pantry staples and some fresh herbs make dinner a snap. Increase the fibre by choosing whole grain pasta, if you like, and top with a sprinkling of grated Parmesan cheese at the table.

12 oz (340 g) **penne pasta**

2 tbsp **extra-virgin olive oil**

2 cloves **garlic,** thinly sliced

1 can (28 oz/796 mL) **diced tomatoes**

¼ tsp **pepper**

¼ cup **black olives,** sliced

¼ cup packed **fresh basil,** sliced

In large pot of boiling salted water, cook pasta until al dente. Reserving ⅓ cup of the cooking liquid, drain; return pasta to pot.

Meanwhile, in large deep skillet, heat oil over medium heat; cook garlic, stirring, until light golden, about 1 minute.

Add tomatoes and pepper; bring to boil. Reduce heat and simmer, stirring occasionally, until slightly thickened, about 8 minutes.

Stir into pasta along with olives and ¼ cup of the reserved cooking liquid, adding remaining liquid as needed until sauce coats pasta. Cook, stirring, for 2 minutes. Stir in basil.

Makes 4 to 6 servings. PER EACH OF 6 SERVINGS: about 281 cal, 8 g pro, 6 g total fat (1 g sat. fat), 48 g carb, 4 g fibre, 0 mg chol, 386 mg sodium, 312 mg potassium. % RDI: 6% calcium, 26% iron, 3% vit A, 32% vit C, 56% folate.

Beef & Mozzarella Baked Rotini

Baked pastas are hearty and satisfying, especially in the cold weather. Serve this tasty rotini with a simple green salad.

1 tbsp **olive oil**

¼ cup chopped **onion**

1 clove **garlic**

1 lb (450 g) **lean ground beef**

4 cups **Simple Tomato Sauce** (below)

1 pkg (454 g) **rotini pasta**

3 cups shredded **mozzarella cheese**

¼ cup grated **Parmesan cheese**

In large skillet, heat oil over medium-high heat; sauté onion and garlic until softened and translucent, about 3 minutes. Add beef; cook, breaking up with spoon, until no longer pink, about 10 minutes. Stir in tomato sauce; reduce heat to medium and simmer until thickened, about 10 minutes.

Meanwhile, in large pot of boiling salted water, cook pasta for 2 minutes less than package directions indicate (pasta will be slightly undercooked). Drain; return to pot.

Toss together pasta, meat sauce, 2 cups of the mozzarella cheese and 2 tbsp of the Parmesan cheese. Spread in 13- x 9-inch (3 L) baking dish; sprinkle with remaining mozzarella and Parmesan cheeses.

Bake in 350°F (180°C) oven until cheese is melted and pasta is bubbly, about 30 minutes.

make your own!

Simple Tomato Sauce

In saucepan, heat ¼ cup olive oil over medium-high heat; sauté ½ cup chopped onion and 2 cloves garlic, minced, until softened and translucent, 3 minutes. Stir in 2 cans (28 oz/796 mL each) whole tomatoes, breaking up with spoon. Stir in 2 cans (5½ oz/156 mL each) tomato paste, 2 cups water, 2 sprigs fresh basil and/or parsley, 2 bay leaves and 1 tsp salt; bring to boil. Cover and simmer over medium-low heat, stirring often to prevent scorching, for 30 minutes. Discard bay leaves, basil and parsley. *(Make-ahead: Freeze in airtight container for up to 1 month.)* **Makes about 8 cups.**

Makes 8 to 10 servings. PER EACH OF 10 SERVINGS: about 448 cal, 24 g pro, 20 g total fat (9 g sat. fat), 42 g carb, 4 g fibre, 59 mg chol, 562 mg sodium, 536 mg potassium. % RDI: 24% calcium, 29% iron, 11% vit A, 25% vit C, 48% folate.

Sausage & Leek Fusilli

Cooking the sausage in the pan first helps flavour the entire dish. Adding some of the pasta water at the end helps to loosen the sauce and coat the pasta without adding any fat.

12 oz (340 g) **fusilli pasta**

2 **mild Italian sausages** (8 oz/225 g total), casings removed

2 tsp **olive oil** (optional)

2 large **leeks** (white and light green parts only), halved lengthwise and thinly sliced crosswise

Pinch each **salt** and **pepper**

¾ cup **sodium-reduced chicken broth**

2 cups **cherry tomatoes,** halved

½ cup grated **Parmesan cheese**

¼ cup chopped **fresh parsley**

In large saucepan of boiling salted water, cook pasta until al dente; reserving ½ cup of the cooking liquid, drain.

Meanwhile, in large skillet, cook sausage meat over medium-high heat, breaking up with spoon, until golden and crisp, about 5 minutes. With slotted spoon, transfer to bowl.

Drain all but 2 tsp fat from pan, or add oil if less than 2 tsp remains. Cook leeks, salt and pepper over medium heat, stirring often, until slightly softened, about 3 minutes. Add broth and bring to boil; reduce heat and simmer until leeks are softened but some liquid remains, about 5 minutes.

Add tomatoes, Parmesan cheese, parsley, pasta, reserved cooking liquid and half of the sausage; cook, tossing, until tomatoes are softened slightly, 2 minutes. Serve topped with remaining sausage.

Makes 4 servings. PER SERVING: about 531 cal, 26 g pro, 15 g total fat (6 g sat. fat), 73 g carb, 6 g fibre, 37 mg chol, 942 mg sodium, 413 mg potassium. % RDI: 18% calcium, 36% iron, 11% vit A, 28% vit C, 93% folate.

Cheesy Baked Sausage-Stuffed Shells

When you need a comfort-food dish to feed a crowd, look no further. Serve these tender, cheesy shells with a salad, and dinner is complete.

32 **jumbo pasta shells**
(one 250 g pkg)

¼ cup **extra-virgin olive oil**

2 each **onions** and **sweet green peppers,** finely diced

4 cloves **garlic,** minced

2 lb (900 g) **mild Italian sausages,** casings removed

2 **eggs**

½ cup chopped **fresh parsley**

1 bottle (680 mL) **strained tomatoes** (passata)

2 tsp **dried oregano**

¼ tsp **salt**

1½ cups shredded **mozzarella cheese**

½ cup grated **Parmesan cheese**

In large pot of boiling salted water, cook pasta until al dente, about 14 minutes. Drain.

Meanwhile, in skillet, heat oil over medium heat; cook onions, green peppers and garlic until softened, about 6 minutes. Transfer to bowl; stir in sausage meat, eggs and parsley, breaking up meat with spoon. Place heaping 1 tbsp sausage mixture in each of the shells. Arrange in greased 13- x 9-inch (3 L) baking dish.

Stir together strained tomatoes, oregano and salt; spoon over stuffed shells. Sprinkle with mozzarella and Parmesan cheeses; cover and bake in 425°F (220°C) oven for 20 minutes.

Uncover and bake until cheese is golden and instant-read thermometer inserted into centre of several shells registers 160°F (71°C), about 10 minutes.

know your ingredients

Strained Tomatoes (Passata)

Jars of this Italian pantry essential come in several sizes. You can use any of the three most common sizes – 660 mL, 680 mL or 720 mL – in this dish with perfect results. The difference won't amount to much in the finished shells.

Makes 8 servings. PER SERVING: about 694 cal, 31 g pro, 42 g total fat (14 g sat. fat), 44 g carb, 3 g fibre, 131 mg chol, 1,306 mg sodium, 481 mg potassium. % RDI: 23% calcium, 42% iron, 11% vit A, 48% vit C, 51% folate.

Spaghetti With Tuna, Tomatoes and Capers

A quick pasta like this, made with fresh in-season tomatoes and pantry ingredients, is ideal for weeknight meals.

4 **plum tomatoes** (1 lb/450 g)

12 oz (340 g) **spaghetti**

¼ cup **extra-virgin olive oil**

¼ cup drained **capers**

½ cup chopped **fresh parsley**

3 cloves **garlic,** thinly sliced

¼ tsp **salt**

¼ tsp **hot pepper flakes**

2 cans (each 6 oz/170 g) **tuna,** drained

Score X in bottoms of tomatoes; plunge into large pot of boiling salted water for 12 seconds. Using slotted spoon, transfer to bowl of ice water; let stand for 20 seconds. Peel off skins; seed, chop and set aside.

In same pot, cook spaghetti until al dente, about 10 minutes. Reserving ¼ cup of the cooking liquid, drain; return pasta to pot.

Meanwhile, in small skillet, heat oil over medium-high heat; cook capers, stirring, for 1 minute.

Add parsley, garlic, salt and hot pepper flakes; cook, stirring, for 2 minutes. Add to pasta along with tomatoes. Add tuna; toss to coat.

Makes 4 to 6 servings. PER EACH OF 6 SERVINGS: about 360 cal, 20 g pro, 11 g total fat (2 g sat. fat), 46 g carb, 4 g fibre, 13 mg chol, 588 mg sodium, 351 mg potassium. % RDI: 3% calcium, 25% iron, 11% vit A, 25% vit C, 60% folate.

CLASSIC
WITH
A TWIST

Ditali in Tomato Chickpea Sauce

Tubelike ditali pasta make perfect little catchers for this chunky sauce. Chickpeas contain plenty of protein and are a tasty alternative to meat in pasta sauce.

2 tbsp **extra-virgin olive oil**

3 cups sliced **mushrooms**

2 cloves **garlic,** minced

1 **onion,** finely chopped

1 can (14 oz/398 mL) **chickpeas,** drained and rinsed

1 can (28 oz/796 mL) **whole tomatoes,** chopped

¾ tsp **salt**

½ tsp **pepper**

½ tsp **dried oregano**

1¾ cups **ditali pasta,** penne pasta or elbow macaroni

2 tbsp chopped **fresh parsley**

¼ cup grated **Parmesan cheese**

Parsley sprigs

In large skillet, heat oil over medium-high heat; cook mushrooms, garlic and onion, stirring occasionally, until no liquid remains and mushrooms are browned, 10 to 15 minutes.

Stir in chickpeas, tomatoes, salt, pepper and oregano; bring to boil. Reduce heat and simmer until slightly thickened, about 5 minutes.

Meanwhile, in large pot of boiling salted water, cook pasta until al dente, about 8 minutes. Drain and return to pot.

Add sauce and chopped parsley to pasta; toss to coat. Serve sprinkled with Parmesan cheese; garnish with parsley sprigs.

Makes 4 servings. PER SERVING: about 406 cal, 15 g pro, 11 g total fat (2 g sat. fat), 65 g carb, 8 g fibre, 5 mg chol, 1,052 mg sodium. % RDI: 17% calcium, 29% iron, 14% vit A, 58% vit C, 60% folate.

Creamy Meatballs & Noodles

If you have time, chill the meatballs in the refrigerator for 10 minutes before frying; they'll hold their shape a little better.

½ cup **fresh bread crumbs**

1 **onion,** grated

1 **egg**

½ tsp each **salt** and **pepper**

¼ tsp **ground allspice**

1 lb (450 g) **lean ground beef** or medium ground beef

1 tbsp **vegetable oil**

3 tbsp **all-purpose flour**

1½ cups **sodium-reduced beef broth**

½ cup **frozen peas**

¼ cup **whipping cream** or 10% cream

4 cups **no-yolk egg noodles**

In large bowl, stir together bread crumbs, onion, egg, salt, pepper and allspice; mix in beef. Shape into 20 meatballs.

In large nonstick skillet, heat oil over medium-high heat; cook meatballs until instant-read thermometer inserted into centre of several reads 160°F (71°C), about 10 minutes. Remove meatballs and set aside.

Drain all but 2 tbsp fat from skillet; whisk in flour. Cook over medium heat, whisking constantly, for 1 minute. Whisk in broth and ½ cup water; bring to boil. Reduce heat and simmer for 3 minutes.

Stir in meatballs; cook until thickened, 3 minutes. Add peas and cream; simmer for 1 minute.

Meanwhile, in large pot of boiling salted water, cook noodles according to package directions. Drain; serve topped with meatball mixture.

Makes 4 servings. PER SERVING: about 540 cal, 33 g pro, 26 g total fat (10 g sat. fat), 41 g carb, 4 g fibre, 134 mg chol, 765 mg sodium, 409 mg potassium. % RDI: 5% calcium, 30% iron, 10% vit A, 3% vit C, 57% folate.

Easy Pasta Puttanesca

This weeknight-easy pasta goes together in about five minutes. Have all your sauce ingredients prepped before the pasta hits the water – freshly cooked pasta can get sticky if it stands too long.

12 oz (340 g) **Homemade Fettuccine** (page 162) or other long pasta

⅓ cup **extra-virgin olive oil**

2 cloves **garlic,** minced

3 **anchovy fillets,** mashed

¼ tsp **hot pepper flakes**

¼ tsp **pepper**

Pinch **salt**

½ cup chopped **fresh parsley**

⅓ cup chopped **Kalamata olives**

½ cup grated **Romano cheese**

In large pot of boiling salted water, cook pasta until tender, about 2 minutes. Reserving ¼ cup of the cooking liquid, drain.

Meanwhile, in large skillet, heat oil over low heat; fry garlic, anchovies, hot pepper flakes, pepper and salt until anchovies dissolve, 1 to 2 minutes.

Add parsley and olives; cook until heated through, about 1 minute.

Add pasta and reserved cooking liquid; toss to combine. Sprinkle with Romano cheese.

know your ingredients

The Right Pasta for the Sauce

This oil-based sauce is best with long pasta, such as fettuccine, linguine, spaghetti or bucatini. Shorter, ridged pastas are better with chunky sauces that need a substantial partner.

Makes 4 servings. PER SERVING: about 535 cal, 17 g pro, 30 g total fat (6 g sat. fat), 50 g carb, 3 g fibre, 155 mg chol, 1,027 mg sodium. % RDI: 17% calcium, 31% iron, 14% vit A, 15% vit C, 71% folate.

Pasta Shells in Double Cheese Sauce

Parmesan gives a rich depth to this simple macaroni and cheese dinner. For a fresh twist, add a spoonful of your favourite salsa at the table.

12 oz (340 g) **small shell pasta**

2 tbsp **butter**

3 tbsp **all-purpose flour**

2 cups **milk**

½ tsp **salt**

¼ tsp each **pepper** and **dry mustard**

Pinch each **cayenne pepper** and **nutmeg**

1½ cups shredded **old Cheddar cheese**

½ cup finely grated **Parmesan cheese**

1 **green onion,** thinly sliced

In large pot of boiling salted water, cook pasta until al dente; drain and return to pot.

Meanwhile, in saucepan, melt butter over medium heat; stir in flour and cook, stirring, for 1 minute. Gradually whisk in milk, salt, pepper, mustard, cayenne and nutmeg; cook, whisking, until thickened, 6 to 8 minutes. Remove from heat.

Stir in Cheddar and Parmesan cheeses until melted. Add to drained pasta; toss to coat. Sprinkle with green onion.

Makes 4 servings. PER SERVING: about 675 cal, 31 g pro, 27 g total fat (16 g sat. fat), 75 g carb, 4 g fibre, 80 mg chol, 1,056 mg sodium, 330 mg potassium. % RDI: 55% calcium, 28% iron, 24% vit A, 2% vit C, 90% folate.

KIDS LOVE IT!

Budget-Friendly Rice

What Makes It Affordable: Rice is a staple in many cuisines. It's grown all over the world, so there's usually an ample supply. You'll find the best deals on family-size bags at your local grocery store or in bulk bins.

Brown rice can be more expensive than its white counterpart. It's less processed than white rice, which, logically, should make it cheaper, but it has become more popular thanks to the growing interest in including whole grains in fibre-starved western diets. Brown rice also has a shorter shelf life, making it trickier for grocers to store.

Wild rice (which is really a grass, not a grain) and multi-rice blends are more expensive than white rice. But rice doubles in volume when cooked, so a small amount can stretch a long way.

Why It's Good for You: White rice is filling and contains a ton of energy in the form of carbohydrates. Enriched rice is enhanced with vitamins and minerals that are absent in white rice. For the highest nutrient value, though, brown rice is the best bet – it is a source of magnesium, phosphorus, B vitamins and fibre.

Wild rice is a source of protein, vitamin E and a number of essential minerals, so it's another nutritious choice. All rice is gluten-free, so it's a delicious option for people with celiac disease.

Food Safety: White rice and wild rice are shelf stable and can be stored for a year or more in a cool, dark, dry pantry. Brown rice contains natural oils in its bran layer and can go rancid at room temperature over time. Store it in an airtight container in the fridge for up to six months or in the freezer for up to one year.

Uses: Rice on its own makes a perfect side dish. But it's also an incredibly versatile ingredient, so try it in everything from soups to stir-fries to desserts.

Wild rice blends are an interesting mix of textures and tastes, and they make a great addition to your menus. Try brown rice pasta in your favourite noodle-based dishes (just be sure to cook according to package directions to keep it from getting gummy).

Couscous & Cheese-Stuffed Zucchini

This entrée calls for fresh herbs and vegetables that are available all year round, but it's terrific for using up zucchini during gardening season. To make it a side, divide the filling among six to eight small zucchini.

1 tbsp **butter**

2 **shallots,** diced

1 clove **garlic,** minced

1 **tomato,** seeded and chopped

¼ tsp each **salt** and **pepper**

½ cup **vegetable broth**

½ cup **whole wheat couscous**

1 cup shredded **Gouda cheese**

3 tbsp thinly sliced **fresh basil**

1 tbsp each chopped **fresh parsley** and **fresh oregano**

4 **zucchini** (about 1½ lb/675 g total)

In saucepan, melt butter over medium-high heat; cook shallots and garlic until softened, about 3 minutes. Add tomato and pinch each of the salt and pepper; cook for 1 minute.

Add broth and bring to boil; stir in couscous. Cover and remove from heat; let stand for 5 minutes. Fluff with fork. Stir in ⅔ cup of the Gouda cheese, the basil, parsley and oregano.

Meanwhile, trim ends off zucchini; slice lengthwise in half. Using melon baller or spoon, scoop out pulp, leaving scant ½-inch (1 cm) thick walls. Sprinkle with remaining salt and pepper.

Divide couscous mixture among zucchini; sprinkle with remaining cheese. Place on baking sheet and cover loosely with greased foil; bake in 400°F (200°C) oven until fork-tender, 25 to 30 minutes.

Makes 4 servings. PER SERVING: about 248 cal, 12 g pro, 11 g total fat (7 g sat. fat), 28 g carb, 6 g fibre, 41 mg chol, 497 mg sodium, 515 mg potassium. % RDI: 22% calcium, 12% iron, 27% vit A, 18% vit C, 18% folate.

Penne With Smoked Sausage and Broccoli

There are many varieties of and seasonings in smoked sausage, so just choose your favourite for this hearty dish.

2 tbsp **extra-virgin olive oil**

12 oz (340 g) **smoked sausage,** sliced

2 **onions,** chopped

2 cloves **garlic,** minced

1 tsp **dried Italian herb seasoning**

½ tsp each **salt** and **pepper**

1 can (28 oz/796 mL) **whole tomatoes**

¼ cup **tomato paste**

¼ cup chopped **fresh parsley**

4 cups **penne pasta** (12 oz/340 g)

4 cups **broccoli florets**

2 cups shredded **Fontina cheese**

½ cup grated **Parmesan cheese**

In large skillet, heat half of the oil over medium-high heat; cook sausage, stirring often, until browned, about 8 minutes. Using slotted spoon, transfer to bowl.

Drain fat from pan; add remaining oil. Cook onions, garlic, Italian herb seasoning, salt and pepper over medium heat, stirring occasionally, until softened, about 5 minutes.

Add tomatoes and tomato paste, mashing with potato masher; bring to boil. Return sausage to pan; reduce heat and simmer until thickened, about 15 minutes. Stir in parsley.

Meanwhile, in large saucepan of boiling salted water, cook pasta for 7 minutes. Add broccoli; cook until tender-crisp and penne is al dente, about 1 minute. Drain and return to pot.

Add sauce; toss to coat. Transfer to 12-cup (3 L) oval baking dish. *(Make-ahead: Let cool for 30 minutes. Cover and refrigerate for up to 24 hours. Add 10 minutes to baking time.)*

Sprinkle with Fontina and Parmesan cheeses. Bake in 375°F (190°C) oven until bubbly, about 30 minutes.

Makes 8 servings. PER SERVING: about 439 cal, 24 g pro, 19 g total fat (9 g sat. fat), 45 g carb, 4 g fibre, 61 mg chol, 1,204 mg sodium. % RDI: 28% calcium, 54% iron, 27% vit A, 85% vit C, 55% folate.

Rigatoni With Roasted Tomatoes & Beans

Treat yourself to this tasty vegetarian main at the height of cherry tomato season.

1 tbsp **butter**

½ cup **fresh whole wheat bread crumbs**

12 oz (340 g) **rigatoni pasta**

¼ cup chopped **fresh parsley**

½ cup grated **Parmesan cheese**

ROASTED CHERRY TOMATOES:

4 cups **grape tomatoes** or cherry tomatoes, halved

2 cloves **garlic,** sliced

2 tbsp **extra-virgin olive oil**

1 tbsp **red wine vinegar**

1 tsp **dried oregano**

¼ tsp each **salt** and **pepper**

1 can (19 oz/540 mL) **navy beans,** drained and rinsed

ROASTED CHERRY TOMATOES: In 13- x 9-inch (3.5 L) cake pan, toss together tomatoes, garlic, oil, vinegar, oregano, salt and pepper; roast in 400°F (200°C) oven until shrivelled, about 20 minutes. Stir in beans and roast until heated through, about 5 minutes.

Meanwhile, in skillet, melt butter over medium heat; toast bread crumbs, stirring often, until crisp and golden, about 3 minutes. Set aside.

Meanwhile, in large pot of boiling salted water, cook pasta until al dente, about 12 minutes. Drain and return to pot.

Add tomato mixture, parsley and half of the Parmesan cheese, tossing to coat. Serve sprinkled with bread crumbs and remaining cheese.

Makes 4 to 6 servings. PER EACH OF 6 SERVINGS: about 410 cal, 17 g pro, 10 g total fat (3 g sat. fat), 64 g carb, 5 g fibre, 10 mg chol, 665 mg sodium, 497 mg potassium. % RDI: 13% calcium, 29% iron, 13% vit A, 27% vit C, 77% folate.

SEAFOOD
YOU CAN
AFFORD

Spaghetti With Mussel Marinara Sauce

Other seafood is often expensive, but mussels are always a great deal. Serve this elegant main with a salad of baby greens and crusty bread for a low-maintenance dinner for four.

2 lb (900 g) **fresh mussels**

1 tbsp **extra-virgin olive oil**

1 small **onion,** minced

½ cup **white wine**

1 lb (450 g) **spaghetti**

¼ cup chopped **fresh basil** or parsley

MARINARA SAUCE:

1 tbsp **extra-virgin olive oil**

2 cloves **garlic**

1 can (28 oz/796 mL) **whole tomatoes**

1 tbsp **balsamic vinegar**

Pinch each **salt, granulated sugar** and **hot pepper flakes**

1 sprig **fresh basil** (or 3 sprigs fresh parsley)

MARINARA SAUCE: In saucepan, heat oil over medium heat; fry garlic, turning, until golden, about 3 minutes. Remove pan from heat. Add tomatoes, mashing with potato masher. Stir in vinegar, salt, sugar, hot pepper flakes and basil. Return to heat and bring to boil; reduce heat, cover and simmer, stirring occasionally, until thickened, about 30 minutes. Let cool. Transfer to food processor or blender; purée until smooth.

Meanwhile, scrub mussels and remove any beards. Discard any mussels that do not close when tapped. Set aside.

In Dutch oven, heat oil over medium heat; fry onion, stirring often, until softened, 5 minutes.

Stir in wine and marinara sauce; bring to boil. Add mussels; cover and cook until mussels open, about 8 minutes. Discard any that do not open.

Meanwhile, in large pot of boiling salted water, cook spaghetti until al dente, about 8 minutes. Drain well; divide among pasta bowls. Top with mussel mixture; sprinkle with basil.

Makes 4 servings. PER SERVING: about 597 cal, 24 g pro, 11 g total fat (2 g sat. fat), 98 g carb, 7 g fibre, 18 mg chol, 748 mg sodium, 757 mg potassium. % RDI: 11% calcium, 65% iron, 7% vit A, 53% vit C, 121% folate.

Risi e Bisi

Risi e bisi, or rice and peas, is a classic northern Italian dish of creamy rice – much like a soupy risotto. This recipe makes a nice light main course for four or an appetizer for six. Pass Parmesan cheese at the table to sprinkle on top.

3 tbsp **butter**

2 oz (55 g) **pancetta,** diced

1 **onion,** diced

6 cups **sodium-reduced chicken broth** or vegetable broth

1½ cups **short-grain rice,** such as arborio or carnaroli

¼ tsp **pepper**

Pinch **salt**

1½ cups **fresh peas** (about 1½ lb/675 g peas in pods)

½ cup chopped **fresh parsley**

½ cup grated **Parmesan cheese**

In saucepan, melt half of the butter over medium heat; cook pancetta and onion, stirring often, until onion is softened, about 7 minutes.

Add broth, rice, pepper and salt; bring to boil. Reduce heat and simmer, uncovered and stirring occasionally, for 18 minutes.

Stir in peas and parsley; cook until peas and rice are tender, about 4 minutes.

Stir in remaining butter and Parmesan cheese; cover and let stand for 2 minutes. Serve in shallow soup bowls.

know your ingredients

Good Broth = Good Food

Use homemade stock or the best-quality commercial broth you can find to make this dish. Make your broth even more flavourful by simmering the empty fresh pea pods in it, covered, for 20 minutes. Strain, pressing pods.

Makes 4 to 6 servings. PER EACH OF 6 SERVINGS: about 362 cal, 13 g pro, 13 g total fat (8 g sat. fat), 48 g carb, 3 g fibre, 29 mg chol, 823 mg sodium, 213 mg potassium. % RDI: 12% calcium, 9% iron, 13% vit A, 18% vit C, 16% folate.

Vegetarian Singapore Noodles

Curry is the signature flavour of this quick-as-a-wink veggie and noodle dish. Look for rice vermicelli that's about the same width as angel hair pasta.

8 oz (225 g) **extra-fine rice stick vermicelli**

3 tbsp **sodium-reduced soy sauce**

2 tsp **granulated sugar**

2 tbsp **vegetable oil**

2 cups shredded **napa cabbage**

1½ cups cubed drained **firm tofu**

1 **sweet red pepper,** julienned

4 oz (115 g) **snow peas,** julienned

4 **green onions,** thinly sliced

2 cloves **garlic,** minced

4 tsp **curry powder**

1½ tsp each **ground cumin** and **ground coriander**

¼ tsp each **salt** and **pepper**

¼ cup chopped **unsalted peanuts** (optional)

In large bowl, soak vermicelli in warm water until softened and separated, about 5 minutes. Drain and set aside.

Meanwhile, whisk together soy sauce, sugar and ¾ cup water; set aside.

In wok, heat oil over medium-high heat; stir-fry cabbage, tofu, red pepper, snow peas, green onions and garlic for 2 minutes. Add curry powder, cumin, coriander, salt and pepper; stir-fry for 1 minute.

Stir in soy sauce mixture; bring to boil. Stir in noodles, tossing to combine; stir-fry until tender, about 7 minutes. Sprinkle with peanuts (if using).

Makes 4 servings. PER SERVING: about 444 cal, 18 g pro, 15 g total fat (2 g sat. fat), 61 g carb, 5 g fibre, 0 mg chol, 658 mg sodium, 478 mg potassium. % RDI: 20% calcium, 31% iron, 16% vit A, 117% vit C, 32% folate.

Chicken Chorizo Paella

Paella recipes usually call for a long list of ingredients and require a lot of steps. This chicken and sausage version has all the authentic taste without all the fuss.

¼ tsp crumbled **saffron threads**

¾ cup warm **sodium-reduced chicken broth**

1 lb (450 g) **boneless skinless chicken thighs,** cut in bite-size pieces

¼ tsp **salt**

2 tbsp **olive oil**

Half each **onion** and **sweet red pepper,** diced

1 clove **garlic,** minced

1 tsp **tomato paste**

1 cup **arborio rice**

½ cup **dry white wine**

4 oz (115 g) **dry-cured chorizo sausage,** sliced

¼ tsp **smoked paprika** or sweet paprika

2 tbsp minced **fresh parsley**

Stir saffron into broth; let stand for 10 minutes. Meanwhile, sprinkle chicken with salt. In large skillet, heat half of the oil over medium-high heat; brown chicken. Transfer to plate.

Add remaining oil to pan; cook onion and red pepper over low heat until onion is translucent, about 10 minutes.

Stir in garlic and tomato paste; cook for 30 seconds. Stir in rice; cook, stirring, for 1 minute.

Add saffron broth, ¾ cup water, wine, chorizo and paprika. Return chicken to pan; bring to boil. Cover and cook over medium-low heat until rice is tender and no liquid remains, about 20 minutes. Stir in parsley. Let stand for 5 minutes.

Makes 4 servings. PER SERVING: about 536 cal, 33 g pro, 24 g total fat (7 g sat. fat), 44 g carb, 1 g fibre, 119 mg chol, 708 mg sodium, 516 mg potassium. % RDI: 3% calcium, 17% iron, 11% vit A, 50% vit C, 8% folate.

SIMPLER
& EASIER

Roasted Cauliflower Risotto

A few pantry staples and a head of cauliflower turn into an elegant risotto, ideal for a vegetarian entertaining menu.

1 head **cauliflower** (about 2 lb/ 900 g), trimmed and cut in florets

3 cloves **garlic**

3 tbsp **extra-virgin olive oil**

½ tsp **salt**

1¼ cups **vegetable broth** or chicken broth

1 large **shallot,** minced (or ¼ cup minced onion)

1 cup **arborio rice**

¼ cup **dry white wine**

⅓ cup grated **Parmesan cheese**

¼ cup chopped **fresh parsley**

Toss together cauliflower, garlic, 2 tbsp of the oil and ¼ tsp of the salt. Roast on greased baking sheet in 400°F (200°C) oven until golden and tender, 35 to 45 minutes. Mash garlic with fork.

Meanwhile, in small saucepan, bring broth and 1¾ cups water to boil; reduce heat to low and keep warm.

In large saucepan, heat remaining oil over medium heat; cook shallot and remaining salt, stirring occasionally, until golden, about 3 minutes.

Add rice, stirring to coat and toast grains. Add wine; cook, stirring, until no liquid remains, about 1 minute.

Add broth mixture, ½ cup at a time and stirring after each addition until most of the liquid is absorbed before adding more, 18 to 20 minutes total. (Rice should be loose, creamy but not mushy, and still slightly firm in centre of grain.)

Stir in cauliflower, garlic, cheese and parsley.

know your ingredients

Parmesan Cheese

Investing in a wedge of Parmesan is worth every penny, since just a sprinkle of this strong hard cheese packs lots of flavour. But if the price tag is too high, less-expensive grana Padano is a flavourful substitute.

Makes 4 servings. PER SERVING: about 351 cal, 10 g pro, 13 g total fat (3 g sat. fat), 49 g carb, 5 g fibre, 9 mg chol, 678 mg sodium, 297 mg potassium. % RDI: 12% calcium, 9% iron, 6% vit A, 112% vit C, 32% folate.

One-Pot Mustard Chicken & Rice

Juicy chicken, crunchy beans and seasoned rice are an ideal mix for a cool night.

1½ lb (675 g) **boneless skinless chicken thighs,** cubed

¾ tsp each **salt** and **pepper**

2 tbsp **vegetable oil**

1 large **sweet onion,** diced

3 ribs **celery,** sliced

1½ tsp **dried dillweed**

1½ cups **basmati rice**

2 tbsp drained **capers,** chopped

1 cup **sodium-reduced chicken broth**

3 tbsp **Dijon mustard**

2 cups cut **green beans** (1 inch/ 2.5 cm)

⅓ cup chopped **fresh parsley**

2 **green onions** (green parts only), thinly sliced

Sprinkle chicken with ¼ tsp each of the salt and pepper. In large Dutch oven, heat oil over medium-high heat; brown chicken, in batches. Using slotted spoon, transfer to plate.

Add onion, celery, dillweed and remaining salt and pepper to pan; cook over medium heat until light golden, about 8 minutes.

Stir in rice; cook, stirring, for 2 minutes. Stir in chicken and capers.

Whisk together broth, mustard and enough water to make 1¾ cups. Add to rice mixture and bring to boil; reduce heat, cover and simmer for 10 minutes.

Add green beans; simmer, covered, for 5 minutes. Turn off heat; let stand on burner for 10 minutes. Stir in parsley and green onions.

Makes 4 to 6 servings. PER EACH OF 6 SERVINGS: about 404 cal, 28 g pro, 11 g total fat (2 g sat. fat), 47 g carb, 3 g fibre, 94 mg chol, 697 mg sodium, 545 mg potassium. % RDI: 8% calcium, 19% iron, 8% vit A, 25% vit C, 21% folate.

Potato Salad
Niçoise Dinner,
page 237

chapter five

Hearty
Vegetables

Slow Cooker Indian-Spiced Carrot Soup

Spices and pantry staples are the backbone of this soup, which gets its heartiness from inexpensive lentils. Puréeing some of the soup adds body and thickness to the broth.

4 cups diced **carrots**

2 **onions,** diced

2 ribs **celery,** diced

1 cup **dried green lentils**

1 tbsp minced **fresh ginger**

2 cloves **garlic,** minced

1 tsp each **ground cumin, ground coriander** and **chili powder**

½ tsp **turmeric, salt** and **pepper**

Pinch **ground allspice**

2 **bay leaves**

3½ cups **vegetable broth**

¼ cup chopped **fresh cilantro**

In slow cooker, combine carrots, onions, celery, lentils, ginger, garlic, cumin, coriander, chili powder, turmeric, salt, pepper, allspice and bay leaves. Pour in broth and 2½ cups water.

Cover and cook on low for 5 to 8 hours.

Discard bay leaves. Transfer 2 cups of the soup to blender; purée until smooth. Return to slow cooker; stir in cilantro.

Makes 8 to 10 servings. PER EACH OF 10 SERVINGS: about 101 cal, 6 g pro, 1 g total fat (trace sat. fat), 20 g carb, 4 g fibre, 2 mg chol, 421 mg sodium, 393 mg potassium. % RDI: 4% calcium, 17% iron, 84% vit A, 7% vit C, 51% folate.

SLOW
COOKER

Celery Root, Leek & Lentil Soup

Knobby celery root, or celeriac, gives this vegan soup a rich celery flavour. A cup of the soup makes a terrific affordable appetizer for a dinner party.

1 **celery root** (about 1½ lb/675 g)

2 tbsp **olive oil** or vegetable oil

1 tsp **fennel seeds**

5 cups chopped **leeks** (white and light green parts only), about 3 leeks

1½ cups chopped **onion**

1 **bay leaf**

1¼ tsp **salt**

¼ tsp **pepper**

⅓ cup **dried green lentils**

1 tsp **curry powder**

1 tbsp **lemon juice**

Trim, peel and dice celery root to make 4 cups; set aside.

In Dutch oven, heat oil over medium heat; cook fennel seeds, stirring, until fragrant, 1 minute.

Add leeks, onion, bay leaf, salt and pepper; cook, stirring occasionally, until softened, 8 minutes.

Stir in celery root, lentils and curry powder; cook for 5 minutes. Add 6 cups water and bring to boil; reduce heat, cover and simmer until flavourful and lentils and vegetables are tender, 20 to 25 minutes.

Discard bay leaf. Stir in lemon juice.

Makes 6 to 8 servings. PER EACH OF 8 SERVINGS: about 113 cal, 4 g pro, 3 g total fat (trace sat. fat), 21 g carb, 4 g fibre, 0 mg chol, 445 mg sodium, 414 mg potassium. % RDI: 6% calcium, 18% iron, 15% vit C, 31% folate.

Cream of Rutabaga Soup

Any *grand-mère* would love this Quebec classic made from rutabaga, which is confusingly known as turnip in many parts of Canada. Serve with crusty sourdough bread to sop up every last drop.

2 tbsp **butter**

1 **leek** (white and light green parts only), chopped

1 **shallot,** chopped

4 cups chopped peeled **rutabaga** (about 2 lb/900 g)

4 cups **chicken broth**

1 cup **whipping cream**

1 tbsp **liquid honey**

½ tsp **salt**

¼ tsp **pepper**

¼ cup chopped **fresh chives**

In large saucepan, melt butter over medium heat; cook leek and shallot until softened, 3 to 5 minutes. Add rutabaga; cook, stirring, for 5 minutes. Pour in broth; bring to boil. Cover, reduce heat and simmer until rutabaga is very tender, about 25 minutes.

With immersion blender or in blender, purée soup until smooth. *(Make-ahead: Let cool. Refrigerate in airtight container for up to 2 days.)*

Return to clean saucepan. Stir in cream, honey, salt and pepper. Cook until heated through. Serve garnished with chives.

Makes 6 servings. PER SERVING: about 257 cal, 6 g pro, 19 g total fat (11 g sat. fat), 17 g carb, 4 g fibre, 61 mg chol, 791 mg sodium. % RDI: 9% calcium, 9% iron, 18% vit A, 55% vit C, 15% folate.

Beef & Root Vegetable Stew

This hearty, rich stew is also wonderful made with caribou, elk or venison – a bonus if you have a hunter in the family.

1½ lb (675 g) **stewing beef cubes,** or boneless caribou, elk or venison stewing cubes

¾ tsp **salt**

½ tsp **pepper**

2 tbsp **vegetable oil**

2 ribs **celery,** chopped

1 **onion,** chopped

¼ cup **all-purpose flour**

2 cups **sodium-reduced beef broth**

1 cup **red wine**

¼ cup **tomato paste**

2 **bay leaves**

¾ tsp **dried thyme**

1 lb (450 g) **yellow-fleshed potatoes,** peeled and cubed

2 **carrots,** peeled and cubed

2 **parsnips,** peeled and cubed

2 **turnips,** peeled and cubed

Sprinkle beef with salt and pepper. In large Dutch oven, heat oil over medium-high heat; cook beef, in batches and turning occasionally, until browned all over, about 6 minutes. Transfer to plate.

Reduce heat to medium; cook celery and onion, stirring, until softened, about 6 minutes. Stir in flour; cook, stirring, for 1 minute.

Return beef to pan; stir in 2 cups water, broth, wine, tomato paste, bay leaves and thyme. Bring to boil; reduce heat, cover and simmer for 1½ hours.

Stir in potatoes, carrots, parsnips and turnips; return to simmer. Cover and cook until beef and vegetables are tender, 40 to 45 minutes. Discard bay leaves.

Makes 8 to 10 servings. PER EACH OF 10 SERVINGS: about 244 cal, 16 g pro, 10 g total fat (3 g sat. fat), 22 g carb, 3 g fibre, 40 mg chol, 392 mg sodium, 668 mg potassium. % RDI: 5% calcium, 17% iron, 27% vit A, 23% vit C, 19% folate.

Velvety Spinach & Potato Soup

Puréed potatoes make soup silky and creamy without adding extra fat.

¼ cup **butter**

2 **shallots,** thinly sliced

2 cloves **garlic,** minced

½ tsp **salt**

¼ tsp **pepper**

1 lb (450 g) **russet potatoes,** peeled and chopped

3 cups **sodium-reduced chicken broth**

10 oz (280 g) **fresh baby spinach,** trimmed

In large saucepan, melt butter over medium heat; cook shallots, garlic, salt and pepper, stirring occasionally, until softened and light golden, about 4 minutes.

Add potatoes; cook, stirring, for 2 minutes. Add 4 cups water and broth; bring to boil. Reduce heat and simmer, uncovered, until potatoes are tender, 15 to 20 minutes.

Turn off heat. Stir in spinach; let stand on burner for 5 minutes.

In blender, in batches, purée soup until smooth.

Makes 4 to 6 servings. PER EACH OF 6 SERVINGS: about 141 cal, 4 g pro, 8 g total fat (5 g sat. fat), 15 g carb, 2 g fibre, 20 mg chol, 580 mg sodium, 428 mg potassium. % RDI: 7% calcium, 14% iron, 55% vit A, 15% vit C, 33% folate.

Beet & Vegetable Borscht

Caraway seeds add an authentic Eastern European taste to this vibrant soup. Choose round red-skinned waxy potatoes – they keep their shape well.

1 tbsp **vegetable oil**

1 each large **onion** and **carrot,** chopped

2 ribs **celery,** chopped

1 **bay leaf**

Pinch **caraway seeds**

4 **beets** (with greens)

2 large **red-skinned potatoes**

4 cups **beef broth,** chicken broth or vegetable broth

1 can (19 oz/540 mL) **whole tomatoes,** chopped

4 tsp **vinegar**

¼ cup **light sour cream**

2 tbsp chopped **fresh dill**

In large heavy saucepan or Dutch oven, heat oil over medium heat; cook onion, carrot, celery, bay leaf and caraway seeds, stirring often, until onion is softened, about 10 minutes.

Meanwhile, trim stalks from beets. Coarsely chop enough of the most tender leaves to make 2 cups; set aside. Peel and cube beets. Peel potatoes if desired and cube.

Add beets, potatoes and broth to pan; bring to boil. Cover and reduce heat; simmer until vegetables are tender, about 20 minutes.

Add tomatoes; cook for 20 minutes. *(Make-ahead: Let cool. Cover and refrigerate for up to 1 day. Reheat before continuing.)*

Stir in reserved beet greens; cook until tender, about 2 minutes. Add vinegar; discard bay leaf.

Serve garnished with sour cream and dill.

Makes 4 to 6 servings. PER EACH OF 6 SERVINGS: about 153 cal, 6 g pro, 4 g total fat (1 g sat. fat), 26 g carb, 4 g fibre, 1 mg chol, 754 mg sodium. % RDI: 8% calcium, 14% iron, 48% vit A, 37% vit C, 26% folate.

Sweet Potato & Cauliflower Tagine

Serve this vegetable-packed stew over whole wheat couscous. Preserved lemons are a fragrant treat to enjoy with tagines – look for them in Middle Eastern stores.

2 cups **white pearl onions** (10-oz/284 g bag), or 2 onions, cut in wedges

1 tbsp **vegetable oil**

3 cloves **garlic,** minced

1½ tsp **ground cumin**

1 tsp **sweet paprika**

½ tsp **ground ginger**

½ tsp **salt**

¼ tsp **pepper**

¼ tsp **cayenne pepper**

3 cups cubed peeled **sweet potato** (1 large)

1 can (19 oz/540 mL) **chickpeas,** drained and rinsed

1½ cups **vegetable broth**

2 cups **cauliflower florets**

1 cup **frozen peas**

2 tbsp minced **fresh cilantro**

Place onions in heatproof bowl; cover with boiling water. Let stand for 5 minutes; drain and peel.

In large deep skillet or shallow Dutch oven, heat oil over medium heat; fry onions, stirring occasionally, until golden, about 5 minutes. Add garlic, cumin, paprika, ginger, salt, pepper and cayenne pepper; fry, stirring, for 1 minute.

Add sweet potato, chickpeas and broth; bring to boil. Reduce heat, cover and simmer for 5 minutes. Stir in cauliflower; simmer, covered, until almost tender, about 20 minutes.

Add peas; simmer, covered, until heated through. Sprinkle with cilantro.

Makes 4 servings. PER SERVING: about 337 cal, 11 g pro, 6 g total fat (1 g sat. fat), 63 g carb, 10 g fibre, 0 mg chol, 852 mg sodium. % RDI: 8% calcium, 24% iron, 177% vit A, 82% vit C, 55% folate.

SMART
CHOICE

Potato Garlic Chorizo Soup

A hint of Spanish flavour from the sausages makes this soup utterly delicious. Can't find chorizo? Try smoked sausages or kielbasa.

2 **yellow-fleshed potatoes** (about 1 lb/450 g)

2 **chorizo sausages** (about 8 oz/ 225 g), sliced

1 tbsp **extra-virgin olive oil**

1 **onion,** thinly sliced

3 cloves **garlic,** minced

1 tsp **dried thyme**

¼ tsp each **salt** and **pepper**

1 can (28 oz/796 mL) **diced tomatoes**

1 tsp **sweet paprika**

1 **bay leaf**

Peel potatoes. Quarter lengthwise; cut crosswise into ¼-inch (5 mm) thick slices. Set aside.

In large saucepan, cook sausages over medium heat until browned, about 3 minutes. Remove and set aside.

Drain fat from pan; heat oil over medium heat. Cook onion, garlic, thyme, salt and pepper, stirring occasionally, until onion is tender, about 5 minutes. Stir in potatoes; cook, stirring, for 2 minutes.

Add diced tomatoes, paprika, bay leaf and 4 cups water; bring to boil. Reduce heat and simmer for 30 minutes.

Add sausages; simmer until potatoes are tender, about 15 minutes. Discard bay leaf. *(Make-ahead: Let cool for 30 minutes. Refrigerate in airtight container for up to 3 days.)*

Makes 4 servings. PER SERVING: about 384 cal, 17 g pro, 22 g total fat (7 g sat. fat), 31 g carb, 4 g fibre, 45 mg chol, 1,111 mg sodium. % RDI: 8% calcium, 26% iron, 5% vit A, 58% vit C, 12% folate.

Curry Vegetable Barley Soup

This hearty soup has a subtle kick; if you like it hotter, increase the curry paste to 1 tbsp. It thickens as it stands, so add a bit of water when reheating leftovers.

4 tsp **olive oil**

1 **onion,** chopped

1 **carrot,** diced

1 rib **celery,** diced

3 cloves **garlic,** minced

1 tbsp grated **fresh ginger**

1½ tsp **Thai red curry paste**

4 cups cubed peeled **rutabaga** (about 1¾ lb/790 g whole)

4 cups cubed peeled **winter squash** (about 2 lb/900 g whole), such as butternut, buttercup or acorn

½ cup **pot barley**

1 tsp **salt**

¼ tsp **pepper**

12 oz (340 g) **mushrooms,** sliced

3 cups packed **fresh baby spinach**

¼ cup chopped **fresh cilantro**

1 tbsp **lime juice**

In large Dutch oven, heat half of the oil over medium heat; cook onion, carrot and celery, stirring occasionally, until onion is softened, 8 minutes.

Add garlic, ginger and curry paste; cook, stirring, for 1 minute. Stir in rutabaga, squash, barley, salt, pepper and 7 cups water; bring to boil. Reduce heat, cover and simmer, stirring occasionally, until barley is tender, about 40 minutes.

Using immersion blender or in blender, in batches, purée until smooth. Return to pot if using blender.

Meanwhile, in large skillet, heat remaining oil over medium-high heat; cook mushrooms, stirring occasionally, until golden and no liquid remains, 8 to 10 minutes.

Stir mushrooms, spinach, cilantro and lime juice into soup; cook over medium heat until spinach is wilted, about 2 minutes.

how to

Prevent Watery Mushrooms

Cooking the mushrooms on the side gives them a nice golden colour and prevents them from becoming waterlogged in the broth.

Makes 6 servings. PER SERVING: about 194 cal, 6 g pro, 5 g total fat (1 g sat. fat), 37 g carb, 8 g fibre, 0 mg chol, 437 mg sodium, 951 mg potassium. % RDI: 12% calcium, 22% iron, 161% vit A, 62% vit C, 32% folate.

Budget-Friendly Hearty Vegetables

What Makes Them Affordable: People have long depended on cabbages, squashes, potatoes and other root vegetables to stretch their budgets. These vegetables tend to be plentiful just before cold weather sets in, and they store well for the months when fresh greens and other produce are in short supply.

These vegetables are great on their own, but they're excellent for stretching recipes that contain small amounts of meat or other protein. They're one of the best ingredients for feeding a crowd on a small budget.

Why They're Good for You: Vegetables are a large and varied group. But, in general, they are packed with healthy vitamins, minerals and fibre, with little or no fat. Deeply coloured root vegetables, such as sweet potatoes, carrots and beets, are also loaded with natural pigments, such as anthocyanins, carotenoids and bioflavonoids, which are key players in cancer prevention.

The fibre in vegetables, especially hearty winter ones, helps fill you up and keep you feeling full longer. Because they are not as calorie-dense as meats or fats, vegetables can constitute a large part of your diet without making you pack on the pounds.

Food Safety: Root vegetables such as rutabagas, sweet potatoes and turnips keep well in a cool, dark, dry place for several weeks. Carrots, beets and parsnips do best in the produce drawer in the refrigerator.

Store potatoes and sweet potatoes at room temperature, not in the fridge. Keep them in a paper bag (never plastic) in a dark, cool cupboard or pantry. It's important to keep potatoes away from light to prevent solanine from building up in the skins and turning them green; this toxin can cause stomach upset.

Cruciferous vegetables, such as cauliflower, broccoli and cabbage, also keep well. Wrap the whole heads or stalks in towels in plastic bags and refrigerate for up to a couple of weeks.

Uses: Hearty vegetables of all kinds are ideal in soups and stews. Try them roasted or grilled as well – the heat caramelizes their natural sugars and enhances their sweetness. And you can never go wrong with a simple baked or boiled potato.

Sweet Potato Soup With Jalapeño Corn Salsa

A spoonful of flavourful salsa adds zip to this simple sweet potato soup.

1 tbsp **vegetable oil**

1 **onion,** chopped

2 cloves **garlic,** minced

¼ tsp each **salt** and **pepper**

3 **sweet potatoes** (2 lb/900 g), peeled and cubed

4 cups **chicken broth**

TOPPING:

1 cup **frozen corn kernels,** thawed

¼ cup minced **red onion** or green onion

2 tbsp minced **fresh cilantro**

1 tbsp minced **jalapeño pepper**

1½ tsp **lime juice** or lemon juice

¼ tsp **salt**

½ cup **light sour cream**

In large saucepan, heat oil over medium heat; fry onion, garlic, salt and pepper until onion is softened, about 3 minutes.

Add sweet potatoes and broth; bring to boil. Reduce heat, cover and simmer until potatoes are tender, about 20 minutes.

In blender, in batches, purée soup until smooth. *(Make-ahead: Let cool for 30 minutes. Refrigerate, uncovered, in airtight container until cold. Cover and refrigerate for up to 2 days or freeze for up to 2 weeks.)* Return to clean saucepan; heat through.

TOPPING: Combine corn, onion, cilantro, jalapeño pepper, lime juice and salt. *(Make-ahead: Cover and refrigerate for up to 4 hours.)*

Ladle soup into warmed bowls. Top each with spoonful of sour cream; spoon corn salsa over top of and beside sour cream.

Makes 4 servings. PER SERVING: about 368 cal, 12 g pro, 8 g total fat (2 g sat. fat), 66 g carb, 6 g fibre, 4 mg chol, 1,120 mg sodium. % RDI: 12% calcium, 14% iron, 344% vit A, 74% vit C, 22% folate.

Carrot Potage

This creamy, rustic soup is easy to prepare and actually tastes best the next day. It's terrific to make when carrots are fresh from the garden or market.

1 tbsp each **extra-virgin olive oil** and **butter**

1 lb (450 g) **carrots,** peeled and chopped (4 cups)

4 oz (115 g) **turnip** or rutabaga, peeled and chopped (2 cups)

1 **onion,** sliced

1 large clove **garlic,** sliced

2 **bay leaves**

½ tsp each **salt** and **pepper**

Pinch **dried marjoram** or thyme

2 cups **sodium-reduced chicken broth** or water

1 large **white potato,** peeled and chopped (1½ cups)

4 oz (115 g) crumbled **blue cheese** (such as Bleu Ermite or Bleu Bénédictine)

2 tbsp minced **fresh chives** or parsley

In Dutch oven, heat oil and butter over medium heat. Add carrots and turnip; cook, stirring occasionally, for 5 minutes.

Add onion, garlic, bay leaves, salt, pepper and marjoram; cook, stirring occasionally, until vegetables are softened but not coloured, about 10 minutes.

Stir in broth and 4 cups warm water; cover and bring to boil. Add potato; reduce heat and simmer, covered, for 30 minutes. Let cool slightly. Discard bay leaves.

In blender, in batches, purée soup until smooth. Strain through sieve into clean saucepan. *(Make-ahead: Strain into airtight container instead of saucepan; refrigerate for up to 2 days.)*

Return just to boil; reduce heat and simmer over medium heat for 5 minutes, stirring and adding up to ¾ cup warm water, if desired, to thin.

Ladle into bowls; sprinkle with cheese and chives.

Makes 6 servings. PER SERVING: about 190 cal, 7 g pro, 10 g total fat (5 g sat. fat), 20 g carb, 3 g fibre, 19 mg chol, 723 mg sodium. % RDI: 13% calcium, 4% iron, 135% vit A, 17% vit C, 12% folate.

Roasted Roots Salad

Get back to your roots, but don't boil them – roast your in-season winter vegetables instead. Serve with roasted meat, poultry or fish.

1 head **garlic**

4 **beets** (about 1 lb/450 g), peeled

4 **carrots** (or half rutabaga), about 1 lb (450 g), peeled

2 **sweet potatoes** (about 1 lb/ 450 g), peeled

1 **celery root** (or 4 potatoes), about 1 lb (450 g), peeled

3 tbsp **olive oil**

½ tsp each **salt** and **pepper**

DRESSING:

¼ cup chopped **fresh mint** (or 1 tsp dried)

2 tbsp **olive oil**

2 tbsp **balsamic vinegar**

¼ tsp **salt**

Trim tip off garlic and cut beets, carrots, sweet potatoes and celery root into 1-inch (2.5 cm) cubes; place in large bowl. Add oil, salt and pepper; toss to coat. Spread on large greased or foil-lined rimmed baking sheet; roast in 425°F (220°C) oven, stirring once, until tender and potatoes are golden, 45 to 55 minutes.

DRESSING: Squeeze garlic pulp into salad bowl. Add mint, oil, vinegar and salt; mash together. Add vegetables; toss to coat. Serve hot or warm.

Makes 6 servings. PER SERVING: about 247 cal, 4 g pro, 12 g total fat (2 g sat. fat), 34 g carb, 6 g fibre, 0 mg chol, 440 mg sodium. % RDI: 8% calcium, 13% iron, 272% vit A, 37% vit C, 33% folate.

Beet Soup With Smoked Sausage

Warm and comforting, soups like this are designed to take away the chill and leave you satisfied. Kielbasa has a wonderful smoky flavour, but try another favourite smoked sausage if you have it on hand.

2 lb (900 g) **beets**

2 tbsp **butter**

2 ribs **celery,** diced

1 cup diced **carrots**

1 **onion,** diced

2 tsp **dried dillweed**

1 tsp **caraway seeds**

¼ tsp each **salt** and **pepper**

4 oz (115 g) **kielbasa sausage,** diced

½ cup diced peeled **potato**

4 cups **sodium-reduced chicken broth**

2 tbsp **tomato paste**

2 tbsp **lemon juice**

Scrub and trim off stem ends of beets. Place on double-thickness square of foil and drizzle with 2 tbsp water; seal tightly. Bake in 425°F (220°C) oven until tender, about 1 hour. Peel and dice; set aside.

In Dutch oven, melt butter over medium heat; cook celery, carrots, onion, dillweed, caraway seeds, salt and pepper, stirring occasionally, until tender, about 8 minutes.

Stir in kielbasa; cook until golden, about 3 minutes. Stir in potato and beets; cook, stirring, for 1 minute.

Stir in chicken broth, 4 cups water and tomato paste; bring to boil. Reduce heat and simmer until flavours are blended, about 45 minutes. Stir in lemon juice. *(Make-ahead: Let cool for 30 minutes. Refrigerate in airtight container for up to 2 days.)*

Makes 4 to 6 servings. PER EACH OF 6 SERVINGS: about 170 cal, 8 g pro, 7 g total fat (4 g sat. fat), 21 g carb, 4 g fibre, 23 mg chol, 815 mg sodium. % RDI: 6% calcium, 13% iron, 39% vit A, 15% vit C, 47% folate.

Roasted Sweet Potato Soup

This recipe makes more rosemary oil than you need to garnish the soup, so use leftovers over roasted or steamed veggies or in salads.

2 large **sweet potatoes** (about 1¾ lb/790 g), peeled and cubed

2 tbsp **extra-virgin olive oil**

½ tsp **salt**

1 small **onion,** chopped

1 each rib **celery** and **carrot,** chopped

2 cloves **garlic,** minced

1 tsp chopped **fresh rosemary**

¼ tsp **white pepper** or pepper

2 cups **Easy No-Salt-Added Chicken Stock** (page 63) or Roasted Vegetable Stock (below)

8 sprigs **fresh rosemary**

ROSEMARY OIL:

¼ cup **extra-virgin olive oil**

2 tbsp **fresh rosemary leaves** (about 1 sprig)

ROSEMARY OIL: In saucepan, heat oil with rosemary over medium-high heat just until fragrant, 3 minutes. Strain through fine sieve into small bowl. *(Make-ahead: Cover and refrigerate for up to 3 days.)*

Mix sweet potatoes with half each of the olive oil and salt. Roast on baking sheet in 450°F (230°C) oven, stirring often, until tender, about 20 minutes.

Meanwhile, in Dutch oven, heat remaining olive oil over medium-high heat; sauté onion, celery, carrot, garlic, rosemary, pepper and remaining salt until softened, 8 minutes. Add stock, potatoes and 4 cups water; bring to boil. Reduce heat, cover and simmer, stirring, for 20 minutes. Let cool slightly.

In blender, in batches, purée soup until smooth; strain into clean pot. *(Make-ahead: Refrigerate in airtight container for up to 3 days or freeze for up to 1 month.)* Reheat if necessary. Garnish each serving with 1 tsp rosemary oil and sprig of rosemary.

make your own!
Roasted Vegetable Stock

In 2 roasting pans, toss together 6 each carrots, onions and ribs celery, coarsely chopped; 2 cups sliced mushrooms; 6 cloves garlic; and 4 tsp vegetable oil. Roast in top and bottom thirds of 450°F (230°C) oven, switching pans and stirring halfway through, until softened and browned, 40 minutes. Transfer to stockpot. Add 12 sprigs fresh parsley; 15 peppercorns, cracked; and 3 bay leaves. Pour 1 cup water into each roasting pan; heat, scraping up browned bits. Pour into stockpot. Add 14 cups cold water; bring to boil. Skim off foam. Simmer over medium heat for 1 hour. Strain through cheesecloth-lined sieve, gently pressing vegetables. Stir in 1 tsp salt. *(Make-ahead: Let cool for 30 minutes. Refrigerate in airtight container for up to 3 days or freeze for up to 4 months.)* **Makes about 10 cups.**

Makes about 8 servings. PER SERVING: about 179 cal, 3 g pro, 11 g total fat (2 g sat. fat), 19 g carb, 3 fibre, 0 mg chol, 188 mg sodium, 325 mg potassium. % RDI: 4% calcium, 9% iron, 155% vit A, 22% vit C, 6% folate.

HIGH IN
VITAMIN A

Spiced Carrot Salad

Cooking the spices mellows the flavour of this fragrant North African–style salad. You can serve it with any lightly seasoned meat, fish or poultry.

14 **carrots** (about 2 lb/900 g)

1 tbsp **olive oil**

2 **shallots** (or 1 small onion), finely chopped

2 cloves **garlic,** minced

½ tsp each **salt, ground cumin, cinnamon** and **sweet paprika**

Pinch **cayenne pepper**

2 tbsp **lemon juice**

¼ cup chopped **fresh cilantro**

Cut carrots into ½-inch (1 cm) thick diagonal slices. In large pot of boiling salted water, cook until tender-crisp, about 5 minutes. Chill under cold water; drain.

Meanwhile, in large skillet, heat oil over medium heat; cook shallots and garlic, stirring occasionally, until softened, about 3 minutes.

Stir in salt, cumin, cinnamon, paprika and cayenne pepper; cook until fragrant, about 1 minute. Add carrots and lemon juice; toss to coat. Scrape into salad bowl; stir in cilantro.

Makes 4 to 6 servings. PER EACH OF 6 SERVINGS: about 97 cal, 2 g pro, 3 g total fat (trace sat. fat), 18 g carb, 4 g fibre, 0 mg chol, 662 mg sodium. % RDI: 5% calcium, 9% iron, 383% vit A, 8% vit C, 10% folate.

Slow Cooker Thai Pumpkin Coconut Soup

Pumpkin is common in Thai cooking. If you're a fan of heat, add an extra hot pepper. For a hit of colour, sprinkle with sliced red hot pepper before serving.

8 cups cubed peeled **pie pumpkin** or other winter squash (2¼ lb/1 kg)

1 **red onion,** chopped

2 tbsp grated **fresh ginger**

3 cloves **garlic,** chopped

1 small **red hot pepper** (such as Thai bird's-eye), seeded and chopped

1 can (400 mL) **coconut milk**

3 cups **vegetable broth**

2 tbsp **fish sauce**

½ cup chopped **fresh cilantro**

2 tbsp **lime juice**

1 tbsp packed **brown sugar**

In slow cooker, combine pumpkin, onion, ginger, garlic and hot pepper. Pour in coconut milk, broth and fish sauce.

Cover and cook on low for 5 to 8 hours.

Using immersion blender, purée soup until smooth. Stir in cilantro, lime juice and brown sugar.

know your ingredients

Pie Pumpkins

Pie pumpkins are smaller, sweeter and much less stringy than jack-o'-lantern pumpkins. They're seasonal, so you won't find them in grocery stores throughout the year. If they're not available, try butternut squash in this soup.

Makes 8 servings. PER SERVING: about 159 cal, 3 g pro, 10 g total fat (9 g sat. fat), 18 g carb, 3 g fibre, 2 mg chol, 644 mg sodium, 560 mg potassium. % RDI: 4% calcium, 19% iron, 19% vit A, 17% vit C, 13% folate.

Braised Shallot & Squash Stew

Try this comforting harvesttime stew with other favourites, such as rutabaga and carrots, instead of the squash. Top each bowlful with croutons or toasted bread crumbs to add a pleasant crunch.

2 tbsp **olive oil**

3 cups **shallots** (about 1 lb/450 g)

6 cloves **garlic**

2 tbsp **all-purpose flour**

2 tsp crumbled **dried sage**

4 cups cubed peeled **squash**

3 cups **vegetable broth**

½ cup **dry white wine**

¼ tsp each **salt** and **pepper**

2 cans (each 19 oz/540 mL)
    white kidney beans, drained
    and rinsed

¼ cup chopped **fresh parsley**

In large Dutch oven, heat oil over medium heat; cook shallots and garlic until golden, about 7 minutes. Add flour and sage; cook, stirring, for 1 minute. Add squash, broth, wine, salt and pepper; bring to boil.

Cover and simmer over medium-low heat, or cover and cook in 350°F (180°C) oven, until squash is tender, about 30 minutes.

Using potato masher, mash half of the beans. Add mashed and remaining whole beans to pan; cook, uncovered and stirring occasionally, until heated through and sauce is slightly thickened, 5 to 10 minutes. Stir in parsley.

Makes 8 servings. PER SERVING: about 230 cal, 10 g pro, 4 g total fat (1 g sat. fat), 40 g carb, 11 g fibre, 0 mg chol, 627 mg sodium. % RDI: 8% calcium, 19% iron, 55% vit A, 25% vit C, 35% folate.

Russian Salad

Packed with vegetables and topped with a fresh-tasting dressing, this dinner salad is a nice change of pace in the winter, when greens are out of season.

4 large **beets** (optional)

3 **potatoes,** peeled

2 **white turnips,** peeled

3 **carrots**

2 cups bite-size **cauliflower florets**

1 **cucumber**

6 oz (170 g) sliced **ham** (optional)

1 head **Bibb lettuce** or
    romaine lettuce

4 **hard-cooked eggs** (see How-To,
    page 237), quartered

2 tbsp chopped **fresh dill**

DRESSING:

¾ cup **light mayonnaise**

¾ cup **light sour cream**

⅓ cup chopped **fresh chives**
    or green onions

¼ cup **prepared horseradish**

½ tsp each **salt** and **pepper**

In large pot of boiling water, cook beets (if using) until fork-tender, about 20 minutes. Drain and let cool; slip off skins. Cut into cubes.

Meanwhile, in large pot of boiling salted water, cover and cook potatoes and turnips for 10 minutes.

Add carrots; cook, covered, until vegetables are just tender, about 15 minutes. With slotted spoon, transfer to ice water and chill; drain well.

Add cauliflower to pot; cook until tender-crisp, 2 to 5 minutes. Drain and chill in ice water; drain well.

Cube potatoes and turnips. Halve carrots lengthwise. Peel cucumber; cut lengthwise into quarters and remove seeds. Cut carrots and cucumber crosswise on bias into ½-inch (1 cm) thick slices. Cut ham (if using) into thin strips.

DRESSING: In large bowl, combine mayonnaise, sour cream, 3 tbsp of the chives, the horseradish, salt and pepper. Add potatoes, turnips, carrots, cauliflower and cucumber; stir to coat well.

Trim and separate lettuce into leaves; line shallow serving bowl. Top with vegetable mixture. Arrange eggs, beets and ham over top; sprinkle with dill and remaining chives.

Makes 6 servings. PER SERVING: about 300 cal, 10 g pro, 15 g total fat (4 g sat. fat), 33 g carb, 5 g fibre, 139 mg chol, 1,038 mg sodium, 794 mg potassium. % RDI: 13% calcium, 11% iron, 75% vit A, 58% vit C, 37% folate.

Slow Cooker Chicken Stew With Sage Croutons

Coming home to the aroma of this hearty big-batch stew, with its harvest vegetables, is so comforting. There's no browning, so prep is quick and easy.

2 **carrots,** chopped

2 **turnips,** peeled and chopped

1 **parsnip,** peeled and chopped

1 **onion,** chopped

1 lb (450 g) small **red potatoes,** chopped

2 each **bay leaves** and sprigs **fresh thyme**

¾ tsp **salt**

½ tsp each **dried rosemary** and **pepper**

18 **boneless skinless chicken thighs** (3 lb/1.35 kg), quartered

1½ cups **sodium-reduced chicken broth**

1 cup **white wine**

⅓ cup **all-purpose flour**

1 tbsp chopped **fresh parsley**

SAGE CROUTONS:

7 cups **crustless bread cubes**

2 tbsp each **olive oil** and **butter,** melted

½ tsp crumbled **dried sage**

In slow cooker, combine carrots, turnips, parsnip, onion, potatoes, bay leaves, thyme, salt, rosemary and pepper. Top with chicken. Pour in chicken broth and wine.

Cover and cook on low until juices run clear when chicken is pierced, 6 to 8 hours.

Discard bay leaves. Whisk flour with ⅓ cup cold water until smooth; whisk into slow cooker. Cook, covered, on high until thickened, about 15 minutes. Stir in parsley.

SAGE CROUTONS: Meanwhile, toss together bread cubes, oil, butter and sage. Spread on baking sheet; bake in 400°F (200°C) oven until crisp, 12 to 15 minutes. Serve sprinkled over stew.

Makes 6 to 8 servings. PER EACH OF 8 SERVINGS: about 452 cal, 38 g pro, 16 g total fat (5 g sat. fat), 37 g carb, 4 g fibre, 149 mg chol, 695 mg sodium, 913 mg potassium. % RDI: 8% calcium, 28% iron, 37% vit A, 38% vit C, 35% folate.

Cabbage Salad With Warm Bacon Dressing

You can use red or green cabbage or combine both for this mouthwatering salad. The warm dressing gently wilts the cabbage without taking away its snap, and the bacon adds a smoky flavour.

2 slices **bacon**

4 cups thinly sliced **cabbage** (about half)

DRESSING:

¼ cup **beef broth**

2 tbsp **wine vinegar**

2 tsp **granulated sugar**

½ tsp **caraway seeds**, crushed

¼ tsp **pepper**

In skillet, cook bacon over medium-high heat until crisp, about 5 minutes. Reserving fat in pan, drain on paper towel–lined plate; chop coarsely. Place cabbage in salad bowl.

DRESSING: In pan with bacon fat, simmer broth, vinegar, sugar, caraway seeds and pepper over medium heat, stirring, for 2 minutes. Pour over cabbage; toss to coat. Sprinkle bacon over top.

time-saver

Preshredded Cabbage

To speed up prep, you can use the preshredded cabbage that's available in the produce section of your grocery store. Keep in mind, however, that it's a better value to slice it yourself.

Makes 4 servings. PER SERVING: about 69 cal, 2 g pro, 4 g total fat (2 g sat. fat), 7 g carb, 1 g fibre, 5 mg chol, 128 mg sodium. % RDI: 3% calcium, 4% iron, 1% vit A, 55% vit C, 18% folate.

Peanut Jicama Salad

The star ingredient – jicama – provides a crunchy contrast to the creamy dressing. See below to learn more about this terrific tuber.

1 **jicama** (about 12 oz/340 g), peeled

1 **sweet red pepper,** chopped

DRESSING:

¼ cup chopped **fresh cilantro**

¼ cup **smooth peanut butter**

3 tbsp **unseasoned rice vinegar**

2 tbsp **teriyaki sauce**

2 cloves **garlic,** minced

1 tsp each **dry mustard** and **sesame oil**

¼ tsp **hot pepper sauce**

Cut jicama into scant ¼- x ¼-inch (5 x 5 mm) strips, about 2 to 3 inches (5 to 8 cm) long, to make about 4 cups; place in salad bowl. Add red pepper. *(Make-ahead: Cover with plastic wrap; refrigerate for up to 4 hours.)*

DRESSING: Whisk together ⅓ cup warm water, cilantro, peanut butter, vinegar, teriyaki sauce, garlic, mustard, sesame oil and hot pepper sauce. Pour over jicama mixture; toss to coat.

know your ingredients

Jicama

A member of the morning glory family, jicama (pronounced HEE-ka-mah) is an edible root that's popular in Mexican and Asian cooking. It's crunchy, low in calories, slightly sweet and a little bland – perfect for a piquant vegetable salad. Raw and cut into sticks, it's delicious with dips; cooked, it stays crunchy and makes a fresh substitute for water chestnuts. Choose firm, thin-skinned jicamas with unblemished light tan skins and creamy white flesh. If it's fresh, jicama will keep, unwrapped, for up to three weeks in the refrigerator or at cool room temperature. Once cut, jicama should be covered tightly with plastic wrap and used within a week.

Makes 4 to 6 servings. PER EACH OF 6 SERVINGS: about 106 cal, 4 g pro, 6 g total fat (1 g sat. fat), 10 g carb, 3 g fibre, 0 mg chol, 285 mg sodium. % RDI: 2% calcium, 6% iron, 12% vit A, 82% vit C, 19% folate.

Winter Vegetable Cheese Gratin

This hearty casserole comes to the table with some soupy broth that is tasty sopped up with crusty bread. Enjoy it as a meatless meal or with sausages.

1 bunch **leeks** (white and light green parts only)

4 **carrots,** cut in large chunks

Half small head **cauliflower,** cut in florets

2 cups **brussels sprouts,** halved

1 lb (450 g) small **potatoes,** peeled, or large potatoes, peeled and cut in large chunks

Few sprigs each **fresh thyme** and **fresh parsley** (or ½ tsp dried thyme)

1 **bay leaf**

2 tbsp **butter**

1 **onion,** finely chopped

½ tsp **salt**

¼ tsp **pepper**

8 oz (225 g) **Swiss cheese,** shredded

Cut leeks in half lengthwise; wash well. Cut into 3-inch (8 cm) lengths, keeping layers together. Arrange in 13- x 9-inch (3 L) baking dish along with carrots, cauliflower, brussels sprouts and potatoes. With kitchen string, tie thyme, parsley and bay leaf into bundle; nestle into vegetables.

In skillet, melt butter over medium-high heat; sauté onion until golden, about 8 minutes. Stir in salt, pepper and 1½ cups water; bring to boil. Pour over vegetables; cover loosely with foil.

Bake in 375°F (190°C) oven until vegetables are tender, 45 to 55 minutes. Uncover dish and discard herb bundle; sprinkle cheese evenly over vegetables. Bake until cheese is melted, bubbly and beginning to brown, about 15 minutes.

change it up!

Cabbage Cheese Gratin

Instead of the cauliflower and brussels sprouts, try half a head of Savoy cabbage, cut into 6 wedges.

Makes 4 to 6 servings. PER EACH OF 6 SERVINGS: about 277 cal, 13 g pro, 14 g total fat (9 g sat. fat), 27 g carb, 5 g fibre, 49 mg chol, 554 mg sodium, 570 mg potassium. % RDI: 30% calcium, 12% iron, 102% vit A, 73% vit C, 33% folate.

FREEZER
FRIENDLY

Potato Cheddar Perogies

The traditional (and indulgent) toppings of crispy crumbled bacon and sour cream really bring these perogies to life.

Savoury Perogy Dough (page 49)

2 tbsp **butter**

1 **onion,** sliced

FILLING:

1 lb (450 g) **russet potatoes,**
    peeled and cubed

2 tbsp **butter**

⅓ cup finely chopped **onion**

½ cup shredded **Cheddar cheese**

¼ tsp each **salt** and **pepper**

FILLING: In large pot of boiling salted water, cook potatoes until tender, about 15 minutes. Drain and transfer to large bowl; mash well. In saucepan, melt butter over medium heat; cook onion until golden and tender, about 5 minutes. Add to potatoes. Stir in cheese, salt and pepper. Set aside.

Working with 1 portion of perogy dough at a time and keeping remainder covered, roll out on lightly floured surface to scant ¼-inch (5 mm) thickness.

Using 3-inch (8 cm) round cutter, cut into rounds. Place 1 tsp filling on each round. Lightly moisten edge of half of the round with water; fold over filling and pinch edges together to seal. Place on flour-dusted cloth; cover with tea towel. Repeat with remaining dough and filling, rerolling scraps, to make 36 perogies. *(Make-ahead: Freeze in single layer on baking sheet until firm. Transfer to freezer bag; seal and freeze for up to 1 month. Cook from frozen, adding 3 minutes to boiling time.)*

In large pot of boiling salted water, cook perogies, in batches and stirring gently, until floating and tender, about 5 minutes. With slotted spoon, transfer to colander to drain.

In skillet, melt butter over medium heat; cook onion until golden, about 8 minutes. Add perogies; cook until golden.

Makes about 36 pieces. PER PIECE: about 75 cal, 2 g pro, 3 g total fat (1 g sat. fat), 11 g carb, 1 g fibre, 10 mg chol, 142 mg sodium, 55 mg potassium. % RDI: 1% calcium, 4% iron, 2% vit A, 2% vit C, 110% folate.

Sweet Potato Perogies

Inspired by Italian squash ravioli, these nontraditional dumplings have a sweet flavour and velvety texture. They're especially good tossed with fresh sage leaves that have been fried in butter just until the butter turns light brown.

1 lb (450 g) **sweet potatoes,** peeled and cubed

⅓ cup grated **Parmesan cheese**

2 tbsp **unsalted butter**

2 tbsp finely chopped **fresh sage leaves**

¼ tsp each **salt** and **pepper**

Savoury Perogy Dough (page 49)

In large pot of boiling salted water, cook sweet potatoes until tender, about 15 minutes. Drain and mash well. Stir in Parmesan cheese; set aside.

In skillet, cook butter over medium heat until nutty brown and no longer frothy. Add sage; cook until crisp, about 1 minute. Stir into sweet potato mixture along with salt and pepper.

Working with 1 portion of perogy dough at a time and keeping remainder covered, roll out on lightly floured surface to scant ¼-inch (5 mm) thickness.

Using 3-inch (8 cm) round cutter, cut into rounds. Place 1 tsp filling on each round. Lightly moisten edge of half of the round with water; fold over filling and pinch edges together to seal. Place on flour-dusted cloth; cover with tea towel. Repeat with remaining dough and filling, rerolling scraps, to make 36 perogies. (*Make-ahead: Freeze in single layer on baking sheet until firm. Transfer to freezer bag; seal and freeze for up to 1 month. Cook from frozen, adding 3 minutes to cooking time.*)

In large pot of boiling salted water, cook perogies, in batches and stirring gently, until floating and tender, about 5 minutes. With slotted spoon, transfer to colander to drain.

Makes about 36 pieces. PER PIECE: about 65 cal, 2 g pro, 2 g total fat (1 g sat. fat), 10 g carb, 1 g fibre, 8 mg chol, 116 mg sodium, 40 g potassium. % RDI: 2% calcium, 4% iron, 18% vit A, 2% vit C, 10% folate.

Potato Salad Niçoise Dinner

This French bistro classic is a refreshing mix of raw and cooked vegetables.

14 **mini new potatoes,** quartered (about 1 lb/450 g)

2 cups **green beans,** trimmed

3 tbsp **extra-virgin olive oil**

3 tbsp **lemon juice**

1 tsp **Dijon mustard**

½ tsp each **dried basil** and **salt**

¼ tsp **pepper**

2 cups **fresh baby spinach**

1 cup **grape tomatoes,** halved

¼ cup **oil-cured black olives,** halved and pitted

Half **sweet red pepper,** diced

4 **hard-cooked eggs** (see How-To, below), sliced

In large pot of boiling salted water, cover and cook potatoes until almost tender, about 10 minutes. Add green beans; cook until tender-crisp, about 4 minutes. Drain.

Meanwhile, in large bowl, whisk together oil, lemon juice, mustard, basil, salt and pepper. Add potato mixture, spinach, tomatoes, black olives and red pepper; toss to coat. Top with eggs.

how to

Perfect Hard-Cooked Eggs

Arrange eggs in single layer in saucepan; pour in enough cold water to come 1 inch (2.5 cm) above eggs. Cover and bring to boil over high heat. Immediately remove from heat; let stand for 15 minutes. Drain and chill eggs under cold water for 2 minutes.

Makes 4 servings. PER SERVING: about 307 cal, 10 g pro, 19 g total fat (3 g sat. fat), 27 g carb, 5 g fibre, 186 mg chol, 1,004 mg sodium. % RDI: 9% calcium, 21% iron, 41% vit A, 102% vit C, 51% folate.

Potato & Chard Hash With Sunny-Side-Up Eggs

Perfect for breakfast-for-dinner lovers, this hash is a comforting meal for a frosty evening. It also makes a wonderful brunch main dish.

1½ lb (675 g) **mini white potatoes**

2 tsp **olive oil**

1 small **onion,** thinly sliced

1 tbsp **butter**

¼ tsp each **salt** and **pepper**

4 cloves **garlic,** chopped

1 **sweet red pepper,** thinly sliced

3 cups coarsely shredded **Swiss chard** (rainbow or green)

1 cup shredded **extra-old white Cheddar cheese**

4 **eggs**

In large pot of boiling salted water, cook potatoes until fork-tender, about 12 minutes. Drain; let cool slightly and cut into quarters.

Meanwhile, in large nonstick skillet, heat 1 tsp of the oil over medium-low heat; cook onion, stirring often, until softened and caramelized, adding 1 tbsp water to pan if browning too quickly, about 10 minutes. Remove from pan; set aside.

In same skillet, melt butter over medium-high heat; cook potatoes, stirring frequently, until light golden, about 5 minutes. Sprinkle with half each of the salt and pepper. Add garlic and red pepper; cook over medium heat until tender-crisp, about 2 minutes. Add chard and reserved onion; cook until chard is wilted, about 2 minutes. Stir in cheese until melted. Remove from pan and keep warm.

Wipe skillet clean. Add remaining oil; cook eggs over medium heat until whites are set but yolks are still runny, 3 minutes, or until desired doneness. Sprinkle with remaining salt and pepper.

Serve hash topped with eggs.

Makes 4 servings. PER SERVING: about 378 cal, 17 g pro, 20 g total fat (10 g sat. fat), 35 g carb, 4 g fibre, 223 mg chol, 786 mg sodium, 850 mg potassium. % RDI: 24% calcium, 20% iron, 43% vit A, 118% vit C, 24% folate.

Warm Potato Salad With Chorizo

Potato salad becomes a meal with the addition of savoury chorizo.

2 lb (900 g) **yellow-fleshed potatoes** (unpeeled)

3 **hard-cooked eggs** (see How-To, page 237), thinly sliced

2 tbsp **olive oil**

1 **dry-cured chorizo sausage,** sliced

1 **onion,** diced

¾ cup **vegetable broth**

¼ cup **white wine vinegar**

½ cup chopped **green onions**

2 tbsp **grainy mustard**

¼ tsp each **salt** and **pepper**

In large pot of boiling salted water, cook potatoes until fork-tender, 20 to 25 minutes. Drain and let cool enough to handle. Cut into thick slices and transfer to large bowl; add eggs.

Meanwhile, in large skillet, heat oil over medium heat; cook chorizo, stirring occasionally, until browned, 3 to 4 minutes. With slotted spoon, add to bowl.

In same skillet, cook onion, stirring occasionally, until golden, 6 to 8 minutes. Add broth and vinegar; bring to boil. Pour over potato mixture. Add green onions, mustard, salt and pepper; toss gently to coat.

Makes 4 servings. PER SERVING: about 376 cal, 13 g pro, 17 g total fat (4 g sat. fat), 43 g carb, 4 g fibre, 176 mg chol, 1,076 mg sodium, 917 mg potassium. % RDI: 6% calcium, 20% iron, 8% vit A, 42% vit C, 21% folate.

Beet Risotto

Beets aren't the usual risotto addition, but they add an earthy, slightly sweet note to this creamy rice dish. The meat stock takes a little work, but it freezes well and is less expensive (and tastier) than store-bought.

4 **beets**

4 cups **Meat Stock** (below) or
    2 cups each sodium-reduced
    beef broth and water

2 tbsp **extra-virgin olive oil**

¼ cup finely chopped **shallots**

1⅓ cups **short-grain rice,**
    such as arborio or carnaroli

¼ cup **dry white vermouth** or
    white wine

1 tbsp chopped **fresh thyme**

1¼ tsp **salt**

½ tsp **pepper**

⅓ cup grated **Romano cheese** or
    Parmesan cheese

1 tbsp **butter**

Wrap beets in foil; roast in 350°F (180°C) oven until tender, about 1 hour. Peel and cut into ¼-inch (5 mm) cubes to make 3 cups; set aside.

In saucepan, bring stock to boil; reduce heat to low and keep warm.

In large deep skillet, heat oil over medium-high heat; sauté shallots until softened and translucent, about 3 minutes. Add rice, stirring to coat and toast grains, about 2 minutes. Stir in vermouth until absorbed.

Add stock, ½ cup at a time and stirring after each addition until most of the liquid is absorbed before adding more, about 20 minutes total. (Taste before adding last ½ cup of stock; rice should be loose, creamy but not mushy, and still slightly firm in centre of grain.) Add beets, thyme, salt and pepper.

Remove from heat. Stir in Romano cheese and butter; let stand for 2 minutes before serving.

make your own!

Meat Stock

In stockpot, combine 10 cups water; 4 lb (1.8 kg) veal and/or beef soup bones; 1 whole chicken leg; 2 onions, halved; 2 ribs celery; 1 carrot; 1 tomato; 2 bay leaves; and 4 sprigs fresh parsley. Bring to boil, about 10 minutes. Reduce heat to low; skim off scum. Simmer, without stirring, until meat falls off bones, 2½ to 3 hours. Strain; refrigerate until cold. Skim off fat. *(Make-ahead: Freeze in airtight container for up to 1 month.)*
Makes about 8 cups.

Makes 4 to 6 servings. PER EACH OF 6 SERVINGS: about 314 cal, 10 g pro, 9 g total fat (3 g sat. fat), 47 g carb, 2 g fibre, 11 mg chol, 680 mg sodium, 530 mg potassium. % RDI: 8% calcium, 11% iron, 4% vit A, 5% vit C, 32% folate.

EASY
WEEKNIGHT
MEAL

Tuna Salad Potatoes

Who doesn't like a stuffed baked potato, especially when it's so quick to make?
Serve with a tossed salad for a simple meal in the middle of the week.

4 large **baking potatoes**
(about 2 lb/900 g)

2 cans (each 170 g) **solid white tuna,** drained

½ cup diced **roasted red pepper**
or fresh sweet red pepper

¼ cup sliced **black olives**

¼ cup **light mayonnaise**

¼ cup **light sour cream**

1 rib **celery,** diced

¼ cup diced **red onion**

2 tbsp chopped **fresh parsley**

2 tbsp **lemon juice**

½ tsp **salt**

¼ tsp **pepper**

Prick each potato several times; microwave on high, turning halfway through, until tender, about 12 minutes.

Meanwhile, in bowl, combine tuna, red pepper, olives, mayonnaise, sour cream, celery, onion, parsley, lemon juice, salt and pepper; set aside.

Cut X in top of each potato; squeeze to open and separate. Mound tuna mixture onto potatoes.

Place potatoes on rimmed baking sheet; broil, 6 inches (15 cm) from heat, until heated through and edges are crisp and darkened, 5 minutes.

change it up!

Tuna Salad Potato Melts

Follow recipe but broil for 2 minutes. Top each stuffed potato with 1 slice Cheddar cheese; broil until bubbly and golden, about 3 minutes.

Makes 4 servings. PER SERVING: about 338 cal, 22 g pro, 8 g total fat (2 g sat. fat), 46 g carb, 4 g fibre, 28 mg chol, 776 mg sodium. % RDI: 7% calcium, 27% iron, 12% vit A, 107% vit C, 14% folate.

Swiss Chard & Potato Gratin

Swiss chard is a summertime treat, and it's an easy-to-grow garden plant. Serve this gratin when bunches of chard are in season.

2 **potatoes** (about 10 oz/280 g), peeled and quartered

3 tbsp **butter**

½ cup diced **onion**

1 large clove **garlic,** minced

½ cup **all-purpose flour**

3½ cups **milk**

¼ tsp **cayenne pepper**

Pinch each **salt, pepper** and **nutmeg**

⅔ cup shredded **Gruyère cheese**

5 cups shredded **Swiss chard leaves**

⅓ cup grated **Parmesan cheese**

In saucepan of boiling salted water, cook potatoes until tender, 10 to 12 minutes. Drain and let cool for 5 minutes; thinly slice. Overlap in greased 6-cup (1.5 L) gratin dish.

Meanwhile, in saucepan, heat butter over medium heat; cook onion and garlic, stirring occasionally, until softened, about 3 minutes.

Stir in flour; cook, stirring, for 1 minute. Gradually whisk in milk, ½ cup at a time. Whisk in cayenne, salt, pepper and nutmeg. Reduce heat to low; simmer, whisking occasionally, until thickened, 5 to 7 minutes. Stir in Gruyère cheese.

Pour about half of the sauce over potatoes. Top with Swiss chard, pressing to compact. Pour remaining sauce over top. Sprinkle with Parmesan cheese. Bake in 400°F (200°C) oven until bubbly and browned, 20 to 25 minutes.

Makes 4 servings. PER SERVING: about 475 cal, 21 g pro, 25 g total fat (15 g sat. fat), 43 g carb, 3 g fibre, 77 mg chol, 657 mg sodium. % RDI: 53% calcium, 16% iron, 41% vit A, 25% vit C, 25% folate.

Curried Potato Kale Galette

This mélange of potatoes and greens makes a pretty, mouthwatering vegetarian main course or a flavourful side dish.

1 tbsp **vegetable oil**

1 **onion,** finely diced

2 cloves **garlic,** minced

1 tbsp minced **fresh ginger**

1 tsp each **ground cumin** and
    garam masala

½ tsp **turmeric**

½ tsp **salt**

Pinch **cayenne pepper**

8 cups chopped stemmed **kale**
    (about 1 bunch)

4 **potatoes** (about 2 lb/900 g)

¼ cup **butter,** melted

In 8-inch (20 cm) ovenproof nonstick skillet, heat oil over medium heat; cook onion, garlic, ginger, cumin, garam masala, turmeric, salt and cayenne pepper, stirring occasionally, until onion is softened, about 8 minutes.

Add kale; cook, stirring occasionally, until wilted, about 5 minutes. Transfer to bowl.

Meanwhile, peel potatoes. Using mandoline or sharp knife, cut into paper-thin slices. Spread one-third in same skillet; top with half of the kale mixture. Repeat layers once. Top with remaining potatoes, pressing to evenly distribute. Pour butter over top.

Bake in 425°F (220°C) oven until potatoes are tender when pierced with knife, about 50 minutes. *(Make-ahead: Let cool for 30 minutes. Refrigerate in airtight container for up to 2 days.)*

Makes 4 to 6 servings. PER EACH OF 6 SERVINGS: about 250 cal, 5 g pro, 11 g total fat (5 g sat. fat), 36 g carb, 4 g fibre, 20 mg chol, 292 mg sodium. % RDI: 13% calcium, 17% iron, 130% vit A, 168% vit C, 16% folate.

acknowledgments

Managing the creation of a cookbook is a little like being the conductor of an orchestra. I may be waving the baton, but it's the contributions from all the people playing their individual instruments – no matter how grand or how humble – that make the final performance a thing of beauty. I'd like to thank the following people for their hard work in making this book a reality.

● Food director Annabelle Waugh and her team, The Canadian Living Test Kitchen, for their delicious recipes, their excellent advice and their desire to help Canadians cook the most delicious food for the most reasonable price

● Chris Bond, art director extraordinaire, for taking a simple idea and making it look like a million bucks (for a fraction of the cost)

● Photographers Jodi Pudge and Edward Pond, food stylists Adele Hagan and Claire Stubbs, and prop stylist Catherine Doherty for shooting and styling the gorgeous new photographs that bring the recipes to life

● Many more photographers and stylists for creating the other mouthwatering photos in these pages (see page 256 for a complete list)

● Julia Armstrong, copy editor and longtime friend, for poring over the pages of this book and making sure our grammar and style were shipshape

● Editors Jill Buchner and Austen Gilliland for graciously pitching in and doing last-minute proofreads when my eyes were too tired to spot any errors

● Beth Zabloski, future library scientist and current book indexer, for making sure readers can find anything they're looking for in the well-organized index on the following pages

● Sharyn Joliat of Info Access for complete, accurate nutrient analysis

● Random House Canada for distribution and promotion of this book

● The Transcontinental Books team in Montreal – vice-president Marc Laberge, publishing director Mathieu De Lajartre and promotion coordinator Ann Nickner – for working with us to turn rough ideas into beautiful finished cookbooks

● *Canadian Living* publisher Lynn Chambers and editor-in-chief Susan Antonacci for supporting and encouraging our team on this cookbook and much, much more

– Tina Anson Mine, project editor

RECIPES

All recipes were developed by
The Canadian Living Test Kitchen.

PHOTOGRAPHY

Ryan Brook/TC Media: back cover (portrait) and page 5.

Jeff Coulson/TC Media: pages 31, 39, 70, 81, 89, 97, 100, 169, 189 and 239.

Yvonne Duivenvoorden: pages 14, 24, 42, 112, 130, 149, 157, 160, 172, 197, 211, 219, 222 and 230.

Joe Kim/TC Media: pages 55, 92, 152 and 203.

Jim Norton: pages 34, 50, 67, 135 and 144.

Edward Pond: front cover and pages 59, 75, 109, 124, 138, 141, 166, 180, 186 and 214.

Jodi Pudge: back and inside covers (food), spine and pages 4, 6, 7, 8, 9, 11, 19, 23, 28, 47, 56, 57, 78, 105, 106, 107, 117, 120, 127, 154, 155, 165, 185, 192, 200, 201, 206, 227 and 233.

David Scott: pages 84 and 242.

Ryan Szulc: pages 62, 177 and 234.

FOOD STYLING

Julie Aldis: pages 219, 222 and 230.

Andrew Chase: page 234.

Ashley Denton: pages 62, 141 and 177.

Carol Dudar: pages 19, 105, 120 and 242.

Adele Hagan: back and inside covers, spine and pages 4, 6, 7, 8, 9, 11, 28, 34, 56, 57, 67, 78, 106, 107, 117, 135, 154, 155, 165, 185, 192, 200, 201 and 206.

Lucie Richard: pages 14, 24, 84, 130, 149, 160, 180 and 233.

Claire Stubbs: front cover and pages 23, 31, 39, 42, 47, 50, 55, 59, 70, 75, 81, 92, 97, 100, 109, 112, 127, 144, 172, 189, 211, 227 and 239.

Melanie Stuparyk: page 203.

Marianne Wren: page 197.

Nicole Young: pages 89, 152, 157 and 169.

PROP STYLING

Laura Branson: pages 19, 34, 39, 62, 67, 70, 84, 97, 100, 105, 120, 135, 144, 152, 177, 180, 206 and 239.

Catherine Doherty: front cover, back and inside covers (food), spine and pages 4, 6, 7, 8, 9, 11, 14, 28, 31, 42, 56, 57, 59, 75, 78, 89, 106, 107, 109, 112, 117, 141, 149, 154, 155, 157, 165, 169, 172, 185, 189, 192, 197, 200, 201 and 227.

Madeleine Johari: pages 50, 55, 81, 92, 124, 138, 166, 186, 214 and 234.

Karen Kirk: page 203.

Catherine MacFadyen: pages 219, 222 and 230.

Oksana Slavutych: pages 23, 24, 47, 127, 130, 160, 211 and 242.

Genevieve Wiseman: page 233.

OKANAGAN REGIONAL LIBRARY
3 3132 03431 2365